The Quest for Wealth

The Quest for Wealth

6 Steps for Making
Mindful Money Choices

Best Wishes!
James

James R. Langabeer, PhD

Routledge
Taylor & Francis Group

A PRODUCTIVITY PRESS BOOK

First published 2022
by Routledge
605 Third Avenue, New York, NY 10158

and by Routledge
2 Park Square, Milton Park, Abingdon, Oxon, OX14 4RN

Routledge is an imprint of the Taylor & Francis Group, an informa business

© 2022 James R. Langabeer, PhD

The right of James R. Langabeer, PhD to be identified as author of this work has been asserted by him in accordance with sections 77 and 78 of the Copyright, Designs and Patents Act 1988.

Library of Congress Cataloging-in-Publication Data
A catalog record for this book has been requested

ISBN: 978-1-03213-993-7 (hbk)
ISBN: 978-1-03213-992-0 (pbk)
ISBN: 978-1-00323-184-4 (ebk)

DOI: 10.4324/9781003231844

Typeset in Garamond
by Apex CoVantage, LLC

To all my colleagues, clients, and students who have helped me form the foundations of the concepts found in this book and my wife for her loving support. And to my Dad, who inspired me to love finance.

Contents

Acknowledgments

Writing this book was more difficult than I thought it would be but more rewarding than expected. What started with a few concepts turned out to be a framework that I hope impacts thousands more people. I couldn't have done it without a lot of help. I must start by thanking my sweet wife, Tiffany. From reading drafts of the book to helping with the ideas and the graphics, she has been instrumental in helping me get this book finished! I was also afforded great motivation from my mother-in-law, Linda Davis, who encouraged me along the way. A special thanks to my parents and step-parents for making me the person I am today. I am also incredibly grateful for the support of Kristine Mednansky, Senior Editor at Routledge Press, for believing in me and publishing this book. My graphics designer Danielle Morrison was very constructive. I also really appreciate the support of all my colleagues, students, and clients who have helped me formulate the concepts I present here.

About the Author

 **James R. Langabeer, PhD, MBA, ChFC©,** is a decision scientist and endowed professor at the University of Texas Health Science Center. He is also the Founder of Yellowstone Consulting, LLC, where he coaches high-performing leaders to improve decision-making around wealth and money. His financial guidance has been featured numerous times in *Forbes* magazine, and he is a member of the Forbes Business Council. He has been a CEO, entrepreneur, and financial advisor, and his passion is to improve prosperity and reduce wealth inequality for everyone. His research has achieved international prominence, with over 120 publications in leading journals and multiple books. He has regularly appeared on national and regional television and radio networks. James earned his Ph.D. in management and decision sciences from the University of Lancaster in England, an MBA in finance from Baylor University, and an undergraduate degree in business management and economics from the University of Texas, San Antonio. He completed his post-graduate training in financial planning from Boston University. He also holds advanced financial designations as a Chartered Financial Consultant (ChFC®), Certified Management Accountant, and is a Registered Investment Advisor. You can reach him at moneycoach@ dr.com.

Figures

Tables

Introduction

If you picked up this book, then you are joining me in a quest—a quest for wealth. This mission leads to a destination filled with financial freedom, abundant resources, and a renewed spirit. Landmines demarcate the quest in all directions, and there are multiple bridges to cross. Today it is the coronavirus epidemic (COVID-19). Yesterday it was a recession. Tomorrow it might be out of control inflation, a reduction in force, divorce, a health issue, or any number of other challenges. Our brains can also hijack the quest—reflexively thrusting us to do something different than maybe we would if were fully conscious. To thrive on this quest, we need armor, weapons, and allies. Armor will be the practices we must follow, weapons will be the tools you learn, and our allies are the advisers and friends who help enable our new mindset and encourage us along the way.

The journey will not be simple, but we start by asking a simple question: What would life look like if I didn't worry about money? Yes, people are walking among us that do not fret about any financial decision they make. But if you are like most Americans, you are struggling to make ends meet financially. Some of you might be inclined to think that it just doesn't matter. Why bother? You will never get ahead. Debt keeps piling up from interest on credit cards and loans, and you never seem to make any progress. If the idea of becoming wealthy seems unattainable or overwhelming, this book is for you. No matter how much you have (or haven't) saved, invested, or planned and wherever you are currently, today is the day to start this quest towards wealth. The path requires you first to cross a significant threshold, a bridge if you will, known as the "bridge of better choices." Here we develop and improve our money mindset. We start by understanding and changing our brains, and then our wallets will follow.

Crossing this first bridge is challenging. Our brain (or technically, our mind) tries to make sense of things by using patterns and heuristics, basically mental shortcuts designed to help. With most matters, this improves our brain's efficiency, basically using an "energy-efficient" mode to save itself for other more complex tasks by shortcutting others. Most things work out fine, but we need full awareness for others that involve some degree of contemplation. Money matters are one area where we must be fully conscious and awake—or Mindful. For instance, it's tough for most people to honestly imagine what they will be doing after they stop working or estimate how much money they need to accumulate by retirement. Shortcuts might cause us to consider these superficially or to avoid them. Yet these are the very types of questions we must confront to achieve wealth and enjoy financial freedom.

In this quest, you first must stop defeating yourself. Your brain is good at playing (and replaying) negative thoughts, but wealth is attainable only through deliberate financial planning. And, as I will later discuss, we need congruency between the emotional and the analytical sides of our brain. Have people gotten wealthy without careful thought and discipline? Sure, but they are the exception and not the rule. I work on the law of probabilities—you are probably 10× more likely to walk towards wealth with a roadmap than just stumbling upon it randomly. Wealth is not an elusive concept only for the ultra-rich. It is for everyone. With a few simple techniques, we can learn to flex our mind's self-control muscles to tame the emotions and thoughts which often hold us back. You will learn about my Mindful Money Management Model™, a proven proprietary path to help you make quick progress towards wealth. Be prepared for a quest that guides you through 6 steps towards wealth and offers practical tools and strategies to keep you on track.

My Story

Since I was young, my interest has always been in managing money and improving decisions. My first board game was called Stocks and Bonds, a little-known board game played, I am sure, by only a few households! Not Life, Candyland, or Clue. Stocks and Bonds. At age eight, I had my first bank account and loved to see my deposits in the old-school check register. My father was a Certified Public Accountant, a saver by nature. My mother is more emotional and less analytical. My childhood, as I recall, was primarily based on hand-me-downs from my older sister and the philosophy of "waste not, want not," as my father used to say routinely.

Armed with my love of money and finance, I studied and earned an MBA and Ph.D. in business management focusing on decision-making. I've started and led businesses and found my version of wealth. I have worked with, talked to, taught, researched, and coached thousands of people over the years during my career. I have studied good choices and learned from the bad ones. I have made sense of these financial choices and synthesized them into a relatively simple framework that can help you understand which traps you might fall into and how to get out of them.

I also have made my share of bad financial decisions and learned some important lessons. My goal here is to provide the best information to help you find your version of wealth and energize you to take action.

Who Should Read this Book?

I specifically wrote this book for those struggling to make ends meet or just beginning a quest towards wealth. You are never too old, or too young, to adopt better money practices. Regardless of your age, you should find some tips of which you might not have been aware. Millennials, Gen Z, and students will also benefit from reading this to help guide the most formative financial years, those within 5–10 years after entering the workforce. If that describes you, please read this book so that you can get the jump-start needed for wealth. If you are a financial advisor, accountant, or coach who wants to learn more about what clients face, this book will be helpful. If you already have advanced financial knowledge, this book might serve as a refresher on some areas.

Why This Book?

I have noticed that most people are looking for practical ways to improve wealth without enduring a long and theoretical book. Although there are some excellent books on the market, they are a little dated. Some books illustrate concepts or issues without offering a practical path forward. Others are superficial, factually incorrect, too academic, long, or difficult to consume. Several books discuss developing good "habits," an important concept, but they often ignore personal finance, budgeting, and wealth. Most fall short in providing concise, valuable tools and techniques to turn your financial condition around. This book aims to be straightforward, practical, and easy to read and focuses exclusively on making better money choices.

Enjoy reading! Soon you will be on the path to long-term wealth.

Quest

(kwest), noun

1. A journey or mission towards a destination that is difficult to find.
2. A search for something meaningful.

Wealth

(welθ), noun

1. The abundance of financial resources.
2. Financial health.
3. Associated with an opportunistic, abundant, confident money mindset.

Mindful

(maɪnd.fəl), adjective

1. Deliberate actions made with full awareness.
2. Being fully present and aware of our choices.

Investment Disclaimer

The thoughts presented in this book are for general information purposes only. I am not endorsing any specific investments, nor is this book intended to replace individualized investment advice.

CROSSING THE BRIDGE OF BETTER CHOICES

"Wealth is the ability to fully experience life."

Henry David Thoreau

Before starting the 6 steps, we must lay a foundation to cross the first significant threshold—the bridge of better choices. In Part I, we talk about the brain's role in financial decision-making and how certain emotions tend to sabotage our quest. In Chapter 1, we start with defining wealth—what it is, and what it is not. In Chapter 2, we discuss a framework for making better choices. We cover psychology and our brain's impacts on financial behaviors in Chapter 3. Fear, doubt, and uncertainty are sure barriers to our success, so we cover that in Chapter 4. We also address why we haven't been able to reach our destination already. When we have these in place, we should have the tools for successfully crossing the threshold and beginning our journey.

DOI: 10.4324/9781003231844-1

Chapter 1

Wealth

"Someone is sitting in the shade today because someone planted a tree a long time ago."

Warren Buffett

The question I often hear is, "How do I get rich?" If you Google that term, over 1 billion sites claim to show how you can become rich quickly. While we all wish there were one magic pill that would make us have bountiful financial resources, there are very few shortcuts to wealth. But some paths are shorter than others. Yet we have more high net worth individuals (HNWIs, or millionaires) now than ever before, with a reported 24 million worldwide.[1] Only a tiny minority of people just fell into this wealth. For most, it resulted from arduous work, good timing, great support, reasonably good execution, collaboration, and lots of luck. As many people are discovering, through a series of deliberate money choices, achieving wealth is possible and highly likely. We need both rules (or mindful money practices, as I call them) and decision tools. The primary aim of this chapter is to describe wealth and set the stage for better money choices.

The Quest

In the following 12 chapters, we will walk through 6 steps on the path towards wealth. I collectively refer to the route, best practices, and personal decision strategies on the quest for wealth as the *Mindful Money Management Model*™ (or M4 for short). M4 is my proprietary path based on decades of research and

DOI: 10.4324/9781003231844-2

practice in this area. The model shows you how the brain often works to sabotage our financial decisions, but more important, it provides you the path and tools needed to overcome. Moving through these steps will help get you from where you are to where you want to be while avoiding the hazards created by our brains' thoughts and emotions. Each chapter outlines very brief and practical tips to guide you through this journey.

You'll see that a critical concept to achieve wealth lies in our ability to confront uncertainty (risks and fear) and ambiguity (lack of clarity). We learn to recognize our risk and money temperament and adopt financial discipline. Want to know the real secret to wealth?—we are our own worst enemy! Our daily choices can either sabotage our wealth or cultivate it. While very few of us will ever get rich overnight, we can become wealthy over time with minor changes and tweaks to how we view and interact with money choices.

As you will see in the M4 roadmap, the journey has several bridges (conceptual hurdles) you need to cross. These bridges represent changes in our way of thinking, acting, and feeling about money. Once you get started, there will be 6 steps, 2 major bridges, 30 mindful money practices, and 20 critical behavioral traps lining the path. You will also need to avoid the top 10 high-risk financial habits. In the following 12 chapters, we will discuss all of these. Figure 1.1 presents the quest. Prepare yourself by reviewing the way forward.

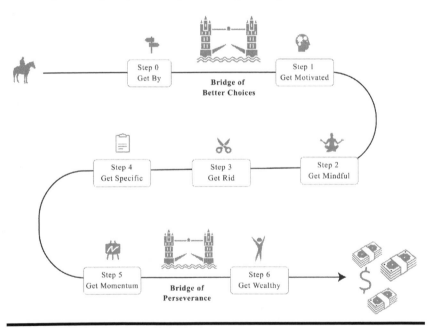

Figure 1.1 The Quest for Wealth.

Wealth

Did you know that people have been on a quest for wealth for over 10,000 years?[2] Well before Indiana Jones started his quest for the Holy Grail. We tend to think that this is a new phenomenon. Some of us might trace it back only as far as Adam Smith's remarkable thesis highlighting how productivity and free markets develop wealth in the same year the United States gained independence as a nation.[3] Why do we all want to achieve some measure of wealth? Well, it affords us freedom—freedom to do more of what we want and less of what we don't. While I am not advocating greedy behavior, I want financial independence and control of my destiny. I am sure if you are reading this book, you do as well.

What do you think of when you hear the word wealth? Money? Rich? Bank? The most straightforward definition of *wealth* is that of an abundance (or over-abundance) of financial resources. From an economic perspective, we calculate wealth as total assets (the things we own) minus what we owe to others (liabilities). In other words, wealth is our marketable *net worth*. Marketable implies that you can sell those assets, and they would convert into cash at some point. Add up all items of value you own and subtract out all that you owe. This concept we will come back to many times. Net worth is one quantitative measure of our financial health.

Sometimes being wealthy is equated with being rich or being famous, but they are not the same. I could be momentarily rich when I win the lottery, but next year after spending it all on new cars and clothes, I will be right back in the same condition. My perspective of wealth suggests four critical qualities: time, behavior, spirit, and relativity.

1. Temporal. Wealth should stand the test of time. It should be sustainable and not just a simple increase in money for a limited time.
2. Behavioral. Wealth determines (and is caused by) how you feel. It has an emotional component and involves more attitude than being simply a concrete financial construct. Emotions impact our perception of whether we have achieved wealth. In this way, I refer to wealth as "financial health."
3. Ethos. Wealth is part of our ethos or spirit. It is not solely an accumulation of money or physical possessions. It has a spiritual connotation relating to our beliefs, values, goals, and aspirations. Our spirit, or *money mindset*, is critical to our quest. We will discuss this multiple times in this book.
4. Relativity. Wealth is relative. We each have our own "version" of wealth. I might feel wealthy with much less in my accounts than my neighbor has. Their aspirations are not your aspirations. Wealth is relative to our own needs, wants, emotions, and lifestyle. We shouldn't compare our wealth, or lack of wealth, with other people; it is only comparable to time and our

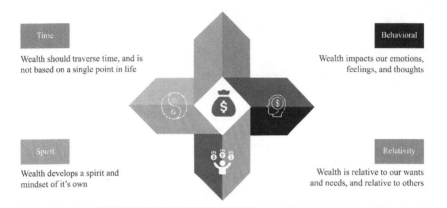

Figure 1.2   The Dimensions of Wealth.

unique aspirations and lifestyle. Therefore, we could achieve our version of wealth with much less money than you might think. When I say "your version" of wealth, I refer to being comfortable with what that looks like for us individually. I don't need $200 million in the bank for my definition of wealth, but I also don't want just $200. Finding the equilibrium level of individual wealth is what remains important in our quest (Figure 1.2).

Wealth involves a combination of all four qualities. It is derived from our emotional comfort and attitude (how we feel about where we are financially speaking) and our relative lifestyle (desired standard of living). When we achieve wealth, we emotionally feel that we have reached sufficient resources and emotional comfort to live our desired lifestyle permanently. Wealth is equal to financial resources plus emotional and lifestyle amenities. Alternatively, I like to view wealth as financial health. You are wealthy if you are financially fit and healthy.

Wealth is relative. Some of us might feel wealthy if we had $10,000 in the bank, while others may have millions and still feel wealth alludes them. At one time, wealth was a magic number—let's say, $1 million. If

Wealth = Financial Health ≠ Rich

you could become a millionaire, you were wealthy. With inflation, some people today think that is not enough. Others believe that is nearly impossible to achieve.

Although the term *high net worth individual* (HNWI) is often used to indicate somebody with a million dollars in marketable net worth, really, there is no specific dollar amount that makes you wealthy. I know of many people who did not have anywhere near $1 million, yet they were comfortable and happy their entire lives. I have had grandparents who had only a small pension and Social Security and felt quite wealthy. It is highly contingent upon your expectations and lifestyle.

Lastly, more is not always better. I still remember that famous movie *Wall Street*, starring Michael Douglas as Gordon Gecko, a New York investment adviser who will do anything to get rich. His favorite quote is something like, "Greed is good. Greed is right. Greed works."[4] He goes on to say that the search for more of everything is the right thing to do. I am not sure that's true since wealth is within our spirit or ethos. Wealth is a spirit of abundance, and we need only enough of it to live the life we are destined for. We don't need more than that. We must set an intention to achieve our version of wealth.

Managing Wealth

In this book, we will walk through the steps towards wealth. The term *wealth management* implies the active, mindful process of growing, preserving, and controlling our financial resources over the long term through mindful and consistent financial decisions. Wealth management is about making rock-solid choices that help you accumulate assets, sustain them, and then direct them to others (should you desire). Sometimes wealth, given its temporal nature, is inter-generational and passed between generations. Those with a significant degree of resources and the ultra-wealthy often leave a financial legacy to benefit future generations. Others are generous with their money and give it to charitable organizations. Other people might want to be wealthy to live financially free and travel the world after retirement.

We all need a reason, a purpose, for any successful journey. Achieving abundance without an intention will not ultimately be fulfilling. Wealth is about the spirit and emotional sides, so you need to go deeper and find your "why" or your purpose. What is your reason for taking this quest?

Mindful Practice 1   Find your "why" for wealth before starting the quest.

Wealth brings about a change in our mindset and outlook and hopefully less stress and anxiety about money. If we are wealthy, we think about being comfortable with where we are. Some of the more common reasons I hear for wanting to become wealthy include:

- More opportunities to do things you have always wanted to do
- Financial prosperity and peace

- Ability to travel more and work less
- Emotional freedom from specific stressors
- Independence from employers and jobs and work structure
- Early retirement

If we focus our minds and behaviors towards achieving wealth, we will need a new mindset. In fact, the first two steps involve finding a healthier money mindset, defining what our money personality type is, and determining what motivates us. As we move into step 3, we get rid of our destructive behaviors. We move from being "afraid" (of losing our jobs, our homes, for instance) to "confident" (that we will survive and make it through any obstacles). If we believe we have options, we can look for the best opportunity to take rather than taking the only one in front of us. Nearly all of us hope to achieve wealth, and so we need to manage it wisely. In step 4, we get focused and financially fit and then can gain momentum in step 5. That will take us to wealth.

Wealth management is a continuous process. It requires a lifetime of making consistent financial decisions, both big and small. I will use the term *decision* throughout to be synonymous with a choice—a selection between alternatives. It requires thinking beyond the present moment and consistently sticking to a plan. But it also requires that you understand principles of sound financial decision-making and a proper sequence of financial choices. Look for the practices, tools, and tips in all chapters to focus on improving our financial decision-making.

Is Wealth Just Luck?

Some people are born rich, like the Rockefellers, Gettys, or Kennedys. In their case, wealth passes from one generation to another—this is what I call a genetic fortune. Unfortunately for us, the number of people becoming wealthy due to an inheritance from a parent or family has declined steadily over the years.[5] You might end up getting a *bequest* (gift or inheritance), but it might be either way too late in life or too small!

Other people get lucky. They might have been in the right place at the right time or just met the right person. You might have won your state lottery or been given money by a long-lost relative or neighbor—I call this serendipitous fortune. And other people have become wealthy because they landed a high-paying job such as a chief executive officer (CEO) or a Wall Street broker.

But research shows that high income can be short-lived and often is quickly wasted if we don't know how to make ongoing wise choices. Think of all the stories of people who won the lottery but then ended up blowing it.[6] Hundreds of stories exist about high-wage earners who made millions but squandered it on bad decisions they later regret. Others have sought out greed through an ongoing quest for more money and ended up with nothing. I have stories from people I work with about never having enough. Others have written some interesting stories about how investors and investment firms can never have "enough."[7] Some people just feel they need more money, more possessions, more property, more of everything relative to the family next door. And that is kind of how we all can be with some things. We just can't get enough _____ (dessert, food, exercise, screen time, movies, sleep, love, downtime . . .). You fill in the blank!

One particular story that stands out to me: my wife and I took a shuttle bus from an airport to our hotel, and we struck up a conversation with the driver. He told us he was a former professional football player who signed with a top team and played professional ball as a defensive lineman for five years. He told stories about the fancy cars, jewelry, dates, and parties and explained how he now has nothing left from those days. Most of us aren't well-trained in how to make continual good choices. That is why he was driving a bus in his late 40s. This situation is not uncommon. Achieving wealth is not the same as maintaining wealth. Our paychecks will eventually go away, so we need without mindful choices to sustain us long-term.

Wealth Is Not a Number

Numbers don't tell the whole story. And numbers are hard to predict. How much do you need to retire, to be comfortable, to stop working? Well, that depends. I can calculate a number for you, given a bunch of assumptions, but there are so many circumstances that it's impossible to predict with any accuracy. Yet financial planners often try to advise clients on identifying a specific number. If you've worked with any, they might ask you to quantify all your needs. Although I love numbers, in my experience, most people have a hard time imagining what their lifestyle will require in the future. That's one of the behavioral traps we have as humans. Most of us are much more driven by how we feel than by a number. We will go through the process of goal setting in Chapter 8, but I will warn you that we likely cannot pinpoint a magic number that will solve all your problems and make you feel wealthy. It is just not realistic. Too many things are uncertain, and too many are unknown. But we can plan for a variety of scenarios.

Mindfulness and Decision Quality

If we go beyond the numbers and understand our purpose for desiring wealth, we must incorporate mindfulness. *Mindfulness* is the deliberate act of being fully present and aware of what we are doing. It requires us to be comfortable with choices we have made, both good and bad, and to recognize that where we are today is not where we will be tomorrow. If we are fully aware, we will not get overwhelmed by the process or our environment, and we will be less like to react rashly. If we are fully mindful, we can begin to see the patterns of choices we might have made. To be *mindful* is to be aware of and conscious of what is happening at the moment. Mindfulness implies complete presence of mind, being fully aware, awake, and conscious of your situation. Mindfulness suggests deliberation, forethought, and reflection. Being mindful about our money choices is precisely the opposite of what we typically do.

Although we like to defend our actions, if we sit with some of the choices we made previously, most of you will be able to view some as "poor" while others you might regard as "good." In reality, we shouldn't judge a decision by the outcome. We can look back at

> **Don't evaluate a decision solely by the outcome.**

any choice over time and talk about how something could or should have been done differently. In football, they call that "armchair quarterbacking." Looking at it from this perspective, we'd say all decisions are probably pretty poor. This fact that we look at life backward reflects a *behavioral bias* (a mental trap or illogical response often made unconsciously, limiting a more thoughtful choice), which we'll discuss in this book. We call it the outcome bias. The *outcome bias* is when we evaluate if our decision was satisfactory based only on the outcome or result rather than assessing it based on what we knew at the time. If we didn't know that a car's airbag was defective when we purchased the car, we can't look back two years later when the vehicle is in an accident and say we made a wrong decision buying that car. At the time we purchased it, we thought we were buying one with working airbags.

The *decision quality* reflects the process we used to choose, given the information we had at the time. Quality is just as important as the outcome. We could have an undesirable effect even if we had all the information in the world, thought about it forever, talked about the choices with 100 experts, and ran the variables through a supercomputer! The outcome may not have been what we wanted, but we did everything we could at the time. Similarly, we could have had a desirable result, but we used a fast, judgmental choice that didn't consider other alternatives. We might have just gotten lucky.

We might want to refrain from calling out choices as "poor" or viewing them as mistakes using this lens. Instead, let's look back at decisions, see a pattern in how we made them, specify what went wrong (or right), and plot how we can get better at choosing over time. That is what I mean by mindful choices. To get better at making mindful choices, we should instead focus on understanding:

- Why we did what we did; was it emotional? Were we pressured?
- Did we have enough information to go on? Did we do research? Was it not balanced? Or not enough?
- What was right (or wrong) with our analyses?
- How we chose to process or analyze it; did we use a spreadsheet; crunch numbers in our head? Just randomly guess?
- How quickly we made a choice. Did we spend time on it? Did we contemplate it? For how long? What was our thought process?
- What level of input we sought from others. Did we consult others?

If we can do that and assess our financial choices afterward, we can learn from our past or continue to do the same thing repeatedly. Using golf terminology, we can't take a "mulligan" or get a second chance at most choices without some form of penalty. Usually, the consequence is that we need to spend more money (like buying something else) or lose time (involved in re-doing what we already once did). If we are fully aware, we might not label our choices, but we definitely can raise them to a level of consciousness. We must bring light to our spending and investing patterns in our past to change it moving forward.

Mindful Practice 2   Look for patterns and problems in your current process of choosing.

WHAT MAKES WEALTHY PEOPLE?

Okay, we might not inherit our wealth or win the lottery, so what makes us wealthy? I see so many infomercials, videos, and books out there that promise to make you rich overnight. You could "flip" houses and make millions even if you have no money or credit. You can buy into a cryptocurrency.

You could be a sponsor or "influencer" and get paid simply to like things. You can be a professional video game player. So many opportunities to get rich quickly! But how many people are really getting rich this way? For the research I conducted for this book, I estimate that less than 1/100 of 1% (or 0.0001) of all wealthy people would fit into any of these categories. It just doesn't happen often, and when it does, it's an exception.

The vast majority of people become wealthy through a combination of good ideas, hard work, years of practice, and rock-solid money choices. Luck, inheritance, gambling, lottery, and Ponzi schemes will not work for 99% of you. A few might get lucky, but most will not. There are very few repeatable (imitable) paths to wealth that can short-circuit this path. However, the good news is that you don't have to make a million dollars per year to become wealthy. In fact, according to most studies of millionaires, the typical million-aire is more likely to be a teacher or government employee than a high-paying CEO.[8]

When making money choices, we rely primarily on the brain's autonomic (more automatic or involuntary) func-tions. We make selections in the moment, often with little or no conscious thought—what to order at a restaurant or what clothes to buy in a store is usually made based on feel-ings and not forethought. This is not a bad thing, but it has to have balance. Mindful money choice involves providing awareness of what is going on inside and around us dur-ing any decision that involves money. What we need is to learn the steps towards making mindful money choices at all times.

Moving Beyond Paycheck to Paycheck

Most Americans are under-prepared financially. One survey by CBS News found that 25% of the population believe they will never get a chance to retire![9] Most people do not even contemplate a path of retirement that does not involve some form of employment. During the typical work career, you will likely work nearly 100,000 hours for a paycheck! Hopefully, this is work that you enjoy doing and are passionate about. Thinking about a career spanning 40–50 years of hard work can be pretty overwhelming. It can also be disappointing if you don't have much to show for it at the end of that journey. Most of us are so busy and absorbed in the daily routine that we lose track of our financial health. Autopilot takes over, often with little thought to our goals and future needs. Sure, we find a way to pay our bills when they come in and might set aside some monthly money in a company retirement account. But did you know that over 95% of consumers have never visited a financial professional to get advice or build a financial plan?[10]

About 90% of us have little to no savings, less than $1,000. Compare that with rates of seeing a medical doctor when you are sick. Over 75% of Americans have a regular primary care physician, who we see routinely.[11] Nearly all of us visit our local mechanic when our automobile breaks down. Yet something as important as your financial health often gets neglected. Whether you are busy operating a chemical plant or managing patients in an emergency department, many of us have no idea how we will possibly be able to retire, let alone become wealthy. Despite perhaps making good salaries for much of that, there is little fruit for this labor.

Now, I am all in favor of living in the moment and enjoying the present moment. That might be all we have. But if an hour or two could help ensure you live a fruitful, wealthy retirement, wouldn't that be worth it? According to one recent survey, nearly 75% of all Millennials believe that the U.S. Social Security program will NOT be there for them when they retire.[12] Couple that with the fact that the average American is nearly $6,200 in credit card debt alone.[13] Nearly 45 million Americans have student loan debt totaling $1.7 trillion (an average of $38,000 per person).[14] Seventy percent of individuals have less than $1,000 in savings to their name.[15] One 2016 report suggests that one in three Americans has $0 saved for retirement.[16] Over 60% of people will likely need to continue working even after their Social Security kicks in because they suffered from one of the multiple behavioral biases I will discuss in this book. Striving to be "regular" like average consumers will only get you into trouble. Strive to be extraordinary.

These are not good statistics. The critical financial metrics around debt and savings for the average household are not getting better. As an optimist, I am confident that the Social Security system will be there for the long term, even if we see a benefit reduction, but this alone is likely insufficient to fund our post-retirement lifestyle. We must be prepared to augment these funds through retirement accounts, investments, and savings.

You might be reading this and are 20 years old and thinking, "Why do I need to think about this now?" Mindful money practices focus more on the future than the present. Focusing on the future will bring you wealth. Learn but don't dwell on the past; this will only lead to regret.

Mindful Practice 3   For each choice, ask yourself: will this improve my future wealth?

CASE IN POINT

Dr. John G. was the department chairman of surgery at a major medical center, with nearly 50 physicians and 100 nurses. He was also a researcher who brought in millions of federal dollars annually to the hospital. He made around $400,000 per year plus bonuses and had a wife and two children. He was highly successful at work and owned a couple of expensive cars and a beautiful home. He assumed that he should be "set" by retirement with as much money as he made—regardless of how he spent or invested. At age 60, after earning nearly $5 million during the previous decade, he had $175,000 in a money market account and $150,000 in a retirement account. The house was worth $1 million but came with a $600,000 outstanding mortgage, and he still had over $100,000 in student loan debt from private medical school. At the same time, that might sound good to many of you, but actually, his rate of savings (or worth) relative to where he should be is pretty poor. Based on his desire to maintain the same style of living, he is not on track for the retirement that he desired.

Wealth Inequality

You might look at the statistics and estimate your probability of becoming wealthy is small. But it doesn't have to be that way. You might never be a billionaire, but you can achieve financial health and wealth if you follow the principles outlined in this book. Yet I don't want to be naïve. There is a well-documented imbalance or disparity in the distribution of money.[17] Older people are more likely to be wealthy.[18] Whites are more likely than Black Americans to achieve wealth.[19] Certain geographic regions are less likely to have HNWIs. But I firmly believe that anybody can overcome inherent inequalities that exist today. It is possible to achieve wealth, regardless of genes, age, geography, or race. We can all do better with our money. Improvement is mainly incremental. If you adopt the tools and techniques in this book, you can make better, lasting choices. I want everyone to become wealthy. Making mindful and consistent financial decisions is essential to overcoming these structural imbalances.

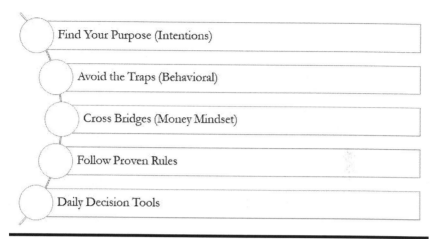

Find Your Purpose (Intentions)

Avoid the Traps (Behavioral)

Cross Bridges (Money Mindset)

Follow Proven Rules

Daily Decision Tools

Figure 1.3   Essential Elements in Our Quest.

The Roadmap to Wealth

In this book, we will discuss a roadmap for wealth. I will introduce you to the six most essential steps to move towards wealth. A significant part of this is the mindset. Our money mindset—the set of attitudes, how we frame and structure our choices, and our philosophy about finances—determines how we behave. Our mindset predisposes us to what kind of car we buy, what neighborhood we move into, and what type of stores we shop. Money mindset determines if we invest, save, or give our money away. We have control over this mindset, and it has to be the first thing we work on if we move from getting by to getting wealthy. Think of layers of a cake, where the foundation has to be the strongest at the bottom. Your mind and outlook are the foundation.

There are five elements you must incorporate into the quest. These elements are shown in Figure 1.3, and we will discuss all of these as we go through the chapters. Please become familiar with these elements so that as you read. You can't just snap your fingers and get these elements in place. It will take work. In the following chapters, we will describe each in more detail.

Take Aways

- To make mindful money choices, we must start with a foundation involving a positive money mindset.
- To achieve wealth, raise the level of awareness of the decision-making process within your mind.

- Mindfulness is essential to wealth development.
- Avoid measuring wealth solely in dollars, given the uniquely emotional element. Since wealth is relative to our unique wants, needs, and lifestyle, we must understand our purpose and intent.
- Our emotions and behaviors essentially drive wealth.
- Follow the five essential elements as you get started on the journey.

Key Terms

behavioral bias, bequest, decision quality, high net worth individual, mindful, mindfulness, mindful money management model, net worth, outcome bias, wealth, wealth management

Chapter 2

Making Better Financial Choices

"It is in your moments of decision that your destiny is shaped."

Tony Robbins

We make more than 100 daily decisions about which direction to turn, what to do with our time, when to pick up and read our phones, and when to eat. We choose what path to drive to work, what train to take, what time to wake up, and even who to listen to on the radio. Of all decisions, the most important ones center around health, wealth, and time. These are our three most valuable assets in decision-making. When all three of these overlap, be prepared to make the single most crucial decision you will probably make in a long time.

In our quest, we are moving towards the "bridge of better choices." This chapter describes the challenges and importance of the financial decision-making process and shows how to make it better to succeed in the journey.

Financial Decisions

Arguably the most pressing choices we make are those that impact our financial resources, our money. A *decision*, or *choice*, represents a selection between two or more alternatives. We nearly always have at least two options: do something or do nothing. But typically, we have many options based on cost, brand, features, benefits, location, and many other things.

DOI: 10.4324/9781003231844-3

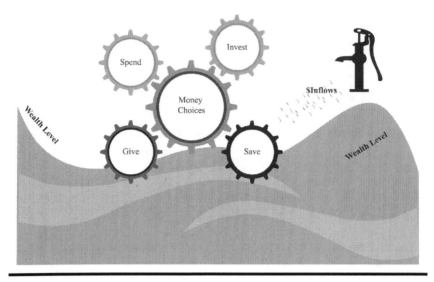

Figure 2.1   Four Categories of Financial Decisions.

Big picture: there are only four primary types of money choices—four big buckets of choices: you could spend, save, invest, or give it away. Part of developing the right money mindset is to keep these money categories in our minds at all times. If we received a $100 gift today from a parent, we could choose to spend it all right now on a new dress. Or we could give it away to a person in need who we meet on the street. Or we could drop it in the bank to save it or invest it later. Each interaction with money is another opportunity to create wealth. It is never too late to turn things around and start making better decisions.

Think about the faucet as our jobs and our investments, which help to bring in new money. The four gears represent what could happen to the new money coming in. The water level represents our wealth, rising and falling based on money in and money going out. Figure 2.1 shows this graphically.

> *Every new day represents a fresh opportunity for better choices.*

Spending

This category is probably the one that we focus more on than the others. Spending includes buying (purchasing), renting, and consuming physical goods as well as utilizing services. It also includes paying our taxes of all types (sales, income, property, franchise) or any other expense. At lower income levels, we have a higher proportionate share of expenditures than in the different categories. That is, those with less disposable income would have a larger spend percentage, generally speaking. Most of the money we make goes out through this category. People spend an average of 75% or more of their income, leaving little for the other types. When you hear people discuss budgets, they typically mean an expense or spending budget rather than a more holistic focus on all four money choices. Spending includes eating at restaurants, buying items on Amazon, going to the bowling alley, or taking a vacation. Spending focuses on "today."

Saving

This category of money choices involves setting money aside for use at a later time. You can save money in a bank account, whole life insurance policy, or under your mattress. Typically, most people choose to place their savings somewhere safe with minimal risk. We'll discuss risk in considerable detail in Chapter 4, but for now, let's assume *risk* equates to potential loss. Therefore, people typically put money in savings to avoid losing any of it, thereby ensuring it will be there in the future, albeit with little growth. Saving focuses on "tomorrow" rather than today.

Investing

This category of money management involves choosing to set money aside for future use while potentially earning an incremental return on that money. Sometimes that return is called interest (on certain types of money market accounts), yields (for bonds as an example), or an increase in future price or asset value (for items that appreciate, for example). Investing in retirement plans, stocks and mutual funds, and real estate are the most common investments you hear people discuss. You might also invest in collectibles or antique cars, assuming the price might increase over time. When we invest, we don't just save, but we account for some *speculation* in what might be a better place to put our money, with the outcome being the future value (rather than the current value). Speculation suggests that while we hope or expect an incremental return in the future, it is not a given, and there are risks involved. Investing has a greater risk than saving, as a general rule, and focuses on "tomorrow" as well.

Giving

Last, the fourth primary money choice is whether (and when) to provide gifts to your children, charitable contributions, non-profit organizations, or other worthy causes. Some people group giving into the spending category, but there is a much more powerful reason many people donate or give money to good causes. The act of generosity or giving (vs. simply spending or consuming) can positively impact your emotions and your brain. Some studies have found that happier people are more generous or that more generous people are happy.[20] Giving also might have a positive impact on our income, surprisingly.[21] It also might have significant tax implications. Giving away focuses more on "others." At certain stages in life, giving might be one of the most important decisions you make.

Mindful Money Management

I am going to use the term *money management* many times in this book. *Money management* plans and controls financial resources, centering on where, when, and how we save, invest, give, and spend our money. To create wealth, we need to become mindful and aware of the mix of dollars allotted to each of these four areas.

This M4 is my proprietary path for making better choices and allocating your income to each of the four money categories described deliberately and intentionally. Part of the discipline of becoming wealthy with limited incoming funds is to optimize (or make the most of) the allocation between categories. Changing the mix will change your results. Think of this in terms of a baking recipe: without a predefined blend of ingredients, the cake will not come out the way you want it; the same with money.

Mindful Practice 4   Take one small step at a time.

Let's dive into this. If we make $1,000 each month, there will be nothing left to save, invest, or give if we spend all $1,000. If we gave it all away, we'd have nothing left to buy our groceries or pay our rent. Without even knowing it, we have an unconscious way of allocating our money between these categories. We learn much of this from watching how our parents handle money. We also might not yet have adequate financial knowledge (or financial literacy). This is also intuitive and reflexive—we automatically make certain decisions without thinking about them.

$$Wealth = f\ (Savings, Investments, Expenditures, Gifts)$$

To be more mindful, we need to bring awareness to it to ensure that you are investing, saving, and gifting in the right proportion to achieve wealth. A simple formula to think about accumulated wealth is adding all of your combined savings and investments (including retirement) and then subtracting all you spend and give. What's left, over time, is your wealth—it is a function of the repeated pattern of choices we make around money.

Consider the graph in Figure 2.2. Imagine two different people; both earn the same salary and have the same level of disposable income. But they make entirely different choices about the mix of how much they will spend versus save, invest, and give. What differs is how they choose to allocate it. Which of the two do you think will accumulate better long-term wealth? If you can contribute a more significant percentage of your paycheck to savings and investments, you will have a much larger nest egg in the future. In this example, the second person has a much smaller proportion of their money contributed towards spending (75% vs. 45%), which frees up more cash for other purposes. Even if that 30% amounted to only $30 per week, $120 extra saved per month would turn into nearly $20,000 in 10 years if invested at only a 5% rate of return. Small dollars saved early grow into wealth.

The heart of financial planning is preparation for an uncertain future. Planning requires consideration not only of your financial decisions and allocations but also of your intentions and aspirations. From a practical perspective, we

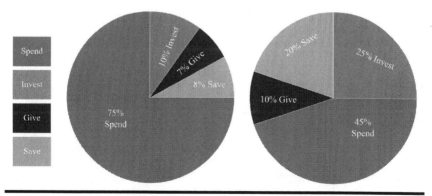

Figure 2.2   Small Changes in Money Allocation Matter.

need to assign budget allocation percentages for each of the four categories and monitor these over time. But we must consider our financial goals, which we will address shortly. Some of these critical money management decisions we face center around these types of questions:

- What do I need to put away for college tuition for my children?
- How much of my income can I spend weekly?
- How much should I save each month for retirement?
- How much mortgage debt can I afford?
- Which credit card should I pay off first?
- When can I retire?
- How much should I save?
- What should my monthly expense budget look like?

Every Decision Matters

Do you remember the largest check you have ever written? Most of us probably can. We can think back and remember the big decisions we have made with money. I remember when I accepted my first full-time job offer and the excitement of knowing that my paycheck would be consistent and nearly triple what I was making as a graduate student. Or remember when you bought that first automobile, took out a mortgage on your first home, or went on an expensive vacation? These major financial choices are relatively rare, though. Much more common are the less expensive, routine decisions you make every single day—things like going out to eat, running to the grocery store, and choosing to buy a coffee versus making it. These are all examples of daily decisions. We make hundreds or thousands of small choices for every big one, yet we often cannot recall any of them.

Our *unconscious* (sometimes also called the subconscious, although there are minor differences) brain tends to make decisions automatically using autonomic processes within the nervous system. In essence, our unconscious brain works on autopilot. Think about how you often wake up and head straight to the bathroom or the kitchen without having to stop and register what you are doing. Or when we drive to work and don't recall shutting the garage door or remembering the names of streets we go down every day.

When we make decisions this way, we have a natural recall bias. The *recall bias is* our inability to remember wholly and accurately what we did in the past.

We are all subject to this bias, and it negatively impacts our money. If we can't recall where our money went unless we use a deliberate process of recording our distributions, then we are making estimates based on guesses. Mindful money processes involve conscious thought and elevating smaller choices to the forefront so that they are understood. When our unconscious minds control our spending, we will have purchased so many small things that we cannot account for at the end of the month even though it drained our cash surplus. That is why it is so important, as we will discuss later, to build a comprehensive budget and track your expenses by category to help you make a better plan.

Mindful Practice 5   Remember that wealth is the sum of all big and small decisions.

CASE IN POINT

Mary and Letitia went out for a few drinks after work one night. At the pub, they wrapped up, and the waiter brought the bill. It was $31.14. Mary instinctively pulled out her credit card and gave it to the waiter within seconds, without even looking at the invoice. Outside, Letitia asked how much the bill was. Mary admitted that she did not even look at it. Think about how often you might be doing the same. Automatic or unconscious processing rarely produces optimal results.

Wealth is the summation of every big and small decision we have ever made, over time. Decisions are all cumulative since we started working and being an adult. It is important to remember that our brains recognize and reward patterns of thinking. When we routinely go on autopilot, our brains reward that pattern, and we are more than likely going to do it the next time we confront a similar scenario. *Patterns* are consistent paths and become engrained in the way we subconsciously just do certain things. When we make a small decision, it becomes part of a pattern of thinking and acting.

In fact, one definition of *financial strategy* is the pattern of financial decisions made over time. Strategy is not the plan you intended but the actual course you took. We might have a good financial plan, but if the choices we make daily don't embrace the plan, then our strategy is much different from the original plan.

When navigating stages of wealth, it is important to focus on how we make these choices and bring light to the way we automatically tend to make small choices without little contemplation. Since choices should always involve selecting between alternatives (more than one potential course of action), we generally should not feel constrained or limited. If we know that there are two things to choose from, it should give us freedom. It should help ensure that we make a choice that improves our result (the *outcome*). Then why does research suggest that people with poorer overall financial health often perceive they have little or no options to choose from? It is easy to think we must do something because we have no other choice. People who are barely "scraping by" believe they are doing the right things with their money; they just don't have enough of it. But even if we have a minimal income, we can always choose to do something, even marginally better, that could improve our financial outcomes.

Start Small

Since we rarely make momentous decisions but instead make multiple small ones daily, we need to improve the process (or system) of decision-making. We tend to under-contemplate more minor expenses relative to the larger ones. Yet small choices add up over a lifetime. Even choosing where and how to spend just $5 per day matters. Some people think, "Well, it's only $5, and you can't buy anything for that." But consider this, even without considering the magic of interest and growth compounding: if you spend just $5 per day every day on something, this will add up to well over $70,000 across 40 years. Considering a growth factor based on rates of return, if you were putting that $5 per day or $150 per month into a mutual fund earning an extremely conservative 3% return per year, you would have nearly $140,000 in your nest egg just from this small incremental savings. Small choices magnify the effect over time. Your patterns of choices divulge where your priorities truly reside. I'm not saying you shouldn't get coffee daily, but I want to highlight that these small purchases add up to big ones over time.

Decision-Making System

So how do you get better at making small decisions daily? We need a system—a common approach, good practices, and work. Practice making good decisions. Bring awareness and deliberation to all aspects of the choice. Focus on framing your mindset and preparing for your finances—document what was happening and why you made that selection. We can learn from the past. First, start by pausing before rushing into any choice. We are usually not pressured to make a speedy choice. Resist the urge that salespeople might place on you, as well as your brain telling you that you must do something right this minute. Pause and breathe. Breathing is a beneficial mindful practice for money. It helps introduce oxygen to our brain, slow down our nervous systems, and bring calmness to the situation. We must make each purchase a more deliberative process, at least while we're learning how to make mindful money choices. Contemplate each option for at least a few seconds before moving forward. We must bring light and exposure to our blind spots. We fall prey to these mental traps without even realizing it. This system of decision-making includes your approach to the choice, the process you used for making it. Contemplative systems for decisions get better over time.

> *Mindful Practice 6 Prepare for the "approach." Pause, breathe, and contemplate before choosing.*

Wealth and Age

Most people follow a typical career life cycle. You might start as a student, graduate, gain employment, begin maturing in that career, and then settle into a long period of working before retirement. This is the age-based life cycle approach to wealth.[22] It assumes that we generally increase our level of wealth over time. This approach identifies three primary periods of wealth management, referred to as

- Accumulation (building wealth)
- Preservation (maintaining wealth)
- Distribution (depleting wealth) (Figure 2.3)

We tend to accumulate assets and money during ages ranging from the 20 to the early 60s. These are our working years. Salaries and wages tend to be at our highest and peak in our 50s. This extended period is known as accumulation because we are focus on accumulating and building wealth (savings and investments). Generally, we begin to consider life after retirement, so our pre-retirement years are focused on preserving as much of our savings and

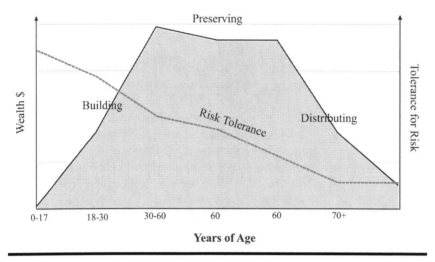

Figure 2.3   Generalized Age-Based Model for Risk and Wealth.

investments as possible, knowing that we will soon not be able to collect monthly paychecks. We spend many years working hard to save and invest so that at some point, we can retire, and when we move into retirement, we often transition into a phase of distribution of our accumulated wealth. We start to spend down some of our savings or individual retirement accounts, usually accompanied by streams of Social Security, which help extend our wealth after retirement. This period of distribution is critical. How much we spend each month and where we have these funds invested determine how long our money will be available.

A real risk for many is that we will outlive our savings. This is called *longevity risk*. On the other hand, most people don't necessarily want to pass away with a large bank account unless they have plans to leave a legacy and contribute their accumulated wealth to others after their death. Either way, life is full of unknowns and uncertainties. We don't know how long we have on this planet or if we will require major expenses such as healthcare or long-term care later in life—so most Americans' goal is to save as much as possible during their lifetimes to protect themselves from this risk. This thinking has a cognitive bias as well.

Yet I think this idea that we all move through the three periods of accumulation, preservation, and distribution is not a complete picture, given the impact of our brains on our decisions. This is the reason behind the mindful money choice framework. We can't just rely on our career phases and age to determine when and if we'll become wealthy! We want wealth earlier, not in our final years. In the next chapter, we will discuss more on how to do this.

Take Away

- We can make more than a hundred choices daily, and most of them are made at the unconscious level.
- Wealth is the summation and accumulation of all decisions, big and small, you've made over time.
- Each time we make a choice, we need to become more mindful.
- Mindful money management involves improving the mix of how we save, invest, spend, and give.
- Raise all decisions to a mindful level to increase our likelihood of future wealth.

Key Terms

decision, financial strategy, longevity risk, money management, outcome, pattern, recall bias, risk, speculation, unconscious

Chapter 3

Brain, Emotion, and Choice

"Do not dwell in the past, do not dream of the future, concentrate the mind on the present moment."

Buddha

Psychology involves the study of how our minds function and process emotions and thoughts. Psychology impacts the path towards wealth, sometimes in ways that are not always clear. Emotions, moods, and even personality traits can sabotage our well-reasoned thought process. The primary aim of this chapter is to show how our impulsive (or emotional) side of the brain often controls our daily financial decisions. Behavioral congruency between the empathic and the analytical side of the brain is needed. I offer a brief introduction to behavioral finance followed by descriptions of the specific impact of moods, feelings, and thoughts on our financial decision-making. Our brains and money have and always will be intertwined. Learn how to recognize and improve your choice process (Figure 3.1).

Psychology of Money Management

We all have a troubled relationship with finances to some extent. *Psychology*—the mental functions performed by the mind and brain—impacts how we think and feel and our actions and behaviors. Many mental health struggles are related

DOI: 10.4324/9781003231844-4

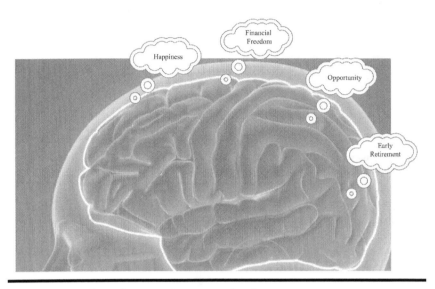

Figure 3.1   Brain and Money Are Intertwined.

to money, whether it's because you don't have enough of it or you have too much. We fight over money. We might hoard it or waste it. We might think it matters more than anything in the world or that it doesn't mean anything at all. Psychological research has shown that our attitudes and behaviors for spending and saving are primarily rooted in our upbringing and genetics. They play out through our thoughts, feelings, and emotions, which interact with the decision-making process.

Psychology partially explains why when we face difficult but not necessarily urgent decisions, we tend to push these thoughts out of our brain subconsciously. We avoid them or make an impulsive choice within milli-seconds. This *autopilot* mechanism—choices made without thought or deliberation—is our brains trying to protect ourselves. It is designed to be efficient and is usually adept at it, but it is just one way our brains influence our money management. Other times we let our emotions and feelings alter the way we spend or invest, and worse of all, we don't even recognize it. Think about how autopilot would shut off on a plane. It happens when a switch is triggered. You should do the same—make sure you turn off autopilot when it comes to money.

I have seen people buy cars, life insurance, and vacation timeshares they didn't need or want just because of the tactics and pressure that good salesman utilize. Good salespeople work on the emotional level, aligning your perceived values and needs with a purchase. We must be trained to overcome these and other behavioral traps that limit our thinking to what we can easily manage in the present moment. These are the kind of questions and statements you need to make when talking to brokers and salespeople:

Is this the best price you can give me?
What else do I need to consider?
Are there other options you haven't told me about?
Is there something else I should be asking you?
I won't be making any choice today, so let me write this down.
I will need some time to think about this.

I call these *behavioral counterforces*—basically other people, your thinking, or anything else that stands in our way of sound decision systems.

Mindful Practice 7 Recognize that others can be behavioral counterforces to mindful money management.

If you are typical of most consumers, then you probably have paid your bills on time, have been able to afford cars and occasional fancy restaurants, and taken family vacations. Most of us gauge our success in managing our finances based on whether we have money still in the bank account at the end of every month. But this is not the right definition of wealth because it doesn't create lasting resource abundance. As we learned, wealth is based on financial freedom and not just having enough money for the current (or present) period. This is *present bias*, in which we more heavily weight alternatives with a smaller benefit or payout "today" rather than a potentially bigger benefit in the future.

Neural Networks

Our brains are so complex. We constantly receive new information, perceive it, process it, store it, and act on it.[23] Recent estimates are that we each have more than 86 billion neurons (or nervous system cells) in our brains.[24] These neurons work together to form connections, resulting in patterns and algorithms called neural networks.[25] *Neural networks* are connections between cells that help our brain learn, store memories, and decide.

We have two primary neural networks which we are focused on: empathic (or what we will refer to hear as emotional) and cognitive (or analytical). The impulsive and empathic side is sometimes referred to as "System 1," and the analytical side as "System 2."[26] In each of us, one side of our brain tends to dominate. Each person though is quite different in how they approach money. The key though, as we will learn, is finding alignment between these two sides of the brain.

Your Analytical Brain

The classical model of financial decision-making process assumes that we are *analytical* or *rational* beings, and when we face a choice, we naturally attempt to understand the problem more and find the best solution. Rational choice assumes that we know what the ideal solution looks like, and we comb through data to find the one that maximizes our *utility*, or benefit.[27] In economics, this is sometimes called classical decision theory. If you are spending money, you would consider all available options, look at prices, and compare all benefits. You would integrate as much data as we can and make an objective choice about value you received versus price paid. That's the theory anyway. Does that sound like you? Some of you it might; for others, I am sure it doesn't fully capture how you think.

For example, if we are buying a car, we tend to look online at prices and specifications. We read reviews, we talk to friends, we drive by car dealerships, and we test drive multiple vehicles. We look up new and used car trading sites to compare pricing. After weeks of this, we make up our mind that we will buy a three-year used SUV, primarily because of the price tag. That all sounds highly rational. We call this *reasoning*, which involves contemplation and consideration of alternatives and consequences. This side of your brain might be more reflective and rule-following. In this regard, think of your brain as a computer. It is more contemplative and deliberate.

What I just described, though, might not be the reality of how our brains work. When we made that big decision to purchase a car in this example, we firmly believed that it was the right choice in our brain. Then we drive down to the dealer and ask for the used car salesman. We look around the showroom while we're waiting. We notice some of the new cars, and we get in. The shiny paint job is beautiful. That new car fragrance is so overwhelming. The salesman walks up and mentions the big sale they are having this weekend on that exact car and that he could put us in it for the same price as the used vehicle we are also considering. Of course, that's on a monthly payment basis, and we'd have to extend our payments from 36 months to 72 months, but it's the same monthly

Figure 3.2   Classical Decision Process.

obligation, right? While finalizing the purchase, the finance manager mentions that we need to protect our investment and purchase tire insurance, window insurance, and possibly paint insurance to protect our investment. Don't we want to manage the risks of our investment? It only adds 1% or 2% to the car's total price, and monthly, this is only $20 extra. So, we end up taking home a brand new four-door sedan instead of a used SUV, with a total sticker price of $51,000 instead of $25,000.

Rational decisions can also be called logical, sensible, or well-thought-out. We start by identifying a need or a want for something. That could be a car, house, new job, or even what restaurant to visit. We then think about what resources we have available. How much do we want to spend? How much time do we have? When does the choice have to be made? We intuitively think through our constraints, such as budget limitations. We then identify alternatives. We could eat out at Restaurant A or Restaurant B, for instance. We weigh the pros and cons of each to evaluate the merits. Then we choose and implement—we do it. It makes perfect sense! Figure 3.2 lays out the classical or rational decision-making process.

But the best-laid plans often turn into different choices than what we initially expected. The ultimate goal we once conceived is so far distant from where we ended up. Why? We don't make decisions in a vacuum, so emotions, behaviors, thoughts, even smells, can get in the way of rational choice. We may not think about long-term consequences from what we consider to be trivial purchases. Also, if you are sad, happy, fearful,

> *Our analytical mind can be helpful, but over-reliance on it can also be harmful. We need judgment.*

stressed, or angry, your ability to rationally think through decisions becomes altered, regardless of whether you can realize it at the moment. The impact of emotions on decision-making is much more common than rationality. With emotions, all of these various factors (stimuli) influence our thought process.

Judgment is our interpretation of the facts, given our past experiences, personalities, and reasoning.[28] Judgment should blend what our hearts and our mind are thinking. Too much of one can overpower the other, creating less than optimal decisions. We should rely on all of our senses and be truly aware of what is happening at the moment of choice.

==

Mindful Practice 8   Cultivate a multi-sensory mindset.

==

Our brain's ability to make financial decisions is influenced by psychology—our thoughts, emotions, and moods all impact our behaviors.[29] *Behavior* is how we act, given what is going on in our brains and the surrounding environment. We need to keep this in check by asking ourselves for each critical decision: am I making the right decision, at the right time? Have I considered all options? There are so many behavioral traps that we can fall into if we're not diligent about recognizing them and avoiding them. That's what this book is about—navigating the stages of wealth while avoiding traps that stand in our way.

CASE IN POINT

Jane B. was a 33-year-old mother of two children. She recently was laid off from her job as an insurance adjuster. While her employer's reviews were generally positive, she was told in the end that if she was more outgoing that her customer satisfaction scores would have been higher, and she might not have been terminated. Since that day, she has had difficulty focusing and is situationally depressed, often feeling down. While she is about to start looking for a new job, she decides that buying something will bring her joy. She ends up buying a $600 bicycle with hopes of beginning to exercise. Two days later, she feels extreme regret over spending money she did not have and wishes that she would have kept the receipt.

Your Impulsive Brain

Daniel Kahneman and Amos Tversky are two extremely famous academic psychology researchers who won the Nobel Prize in Economics for their groundbreaking work on how psychology impacts economic behavior.[30] Their research was the first to show that the way people spend and invest is heavily influenced by psychology and behaviors.[31] In doing so, they created a new field called *behavioral economics,* or *behavioral finance* (I will use the terms synonymously here, although they do have differences). At the fundamental level, both terms reflect the study of our behaviors when making choices involving money. The most noteworthy concept they discovered was that how a problem is framed (or positioned) impacts how individuals decide.[32] They called this *prospect theory*, which suggests that decisions are not always made rationally, given the context in which they are made. Context matters. How we frame, how we perceive, the set of facts presented to us change our choices. This is such a great discovery because it explains why two people presented with identical information would make fundamentally different decisions.

Bounded rationality is another term some researchers have coined to represent the limits of analytical thinking. We either can't compute the right answer or can't fully conceive the problem.[33] This more automatic and impulsive side of the brain is often faster to react, more intuitive, and works at nearly an unconscious level. So behavioral researchers are finding that we aren't entirely as rational as we hoped under normal circumstances.

So, if we know that we don't always behave rationally and are limited in our ability to frame decisions and make optimal choices, how does this impact our ability to do accurate financial planning? This question is the crux of behavioral finance. Our impulses, such as emotions and cognition, often cloud our judgment in ways we don't even know. Anger and fear are the most problematic and potentially destructive of all emotions. Anger can cause us to make more hazardous decisions than we might otherwise, while fear might cause us to avoid decisions altogether. *Emotion* is a psychological state often based on feelings rather than active thought. *Cognition,* however, is the mental process with which we collect, analyze, and act on our thoughts and emotions. Emotion and cognition are tightly linked, and both result in *behavior*, which is the action itself. If we're stressed, we might think we must make a decision, but we have a hesitancy to pull the trigger and feel overwhelmed. If we're sad, we might take less in a negation than we would otherwise. Our cognition (the way we think and perceive the world around us) is formed by experiences, friends, surroundings, and subconscious and even unconscious influences. Figure 3.3 shows a somewhat more realistic decision-making process.

Behavioral Bias

When we make choices around money, our mind does not always process them the same way. Sometimes we rely on unconscious or subconscious control mechanisms to quickly make decisions. When we do, it's easy to fall into behavioral traps or biases. As we mentioned, a behavioral bias is a belief, feeling, or thought that interferes with our more rational decision-making process. There

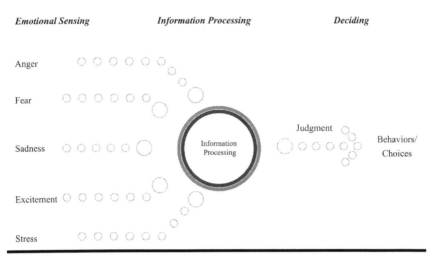

Figure 3.3   More Realistic Decision Process.

are two dominant types: (1) biases or errors in our thinking and judgment (cognitive biases) and (2) feelings and beliefs (emotional biases). Think of a bias as a cage where our thinking confines us. Sometimes we refer to bias as a *fallacy*, a financial untruth. Or they could be stereotypes. We *stereotype* people or objects when we create an idea about them without actually knowing them. We often fall into traps of all forms. For example, we might think that "all doctors are rich" or "I will never get wealthy." These are just behavioral biases that limit our thinking.

Remember that our thinking controls our behavior. Our actions follow our thoughts. If we think we are limited, we will be. We must get rid of the entrapments to see more clearly. That's easier said than done.

This is the impact of behaviors and emotions in financial decision-making. If we recognize it, we might be able to take action and do something about it. Realizing where and when our thinking is flawed could ultimately improve our financial decision processes.

Emotions and Financial Decisions

Money brings out the best and worst in people. Money is a source of fear, stress, worry, and anxiety. Ken Honda's book on "happy money" describes money as "energy," which can be either happy or unhappy.[34] I love this definition since money often serves as the motivation for many people. But I prefer to think about money as emotion and spirit.

Our feelings and emotions drive our thinking. My research on organizational chief executive officers examined the relationship between how optimistic (or confident) they were about their company's future outlook and assessed their level of optimism against their financial performance.[35] Optimism and pessimism are opposing perspectives of genetic predisposition or personality traits. To some degree, you cannot alter your general predispositions. Optimism is a general state of a positive outlook for the future, while pessimism is a general negative outlook on life and your future. My findings are that the more generally optimistic leaders had better financial performance, while the pessimists had a lower overall performance. Those who were more optimistic were more likely to spend more money and make larger purchases in the immediate future. Those who were more pessimistic were more likely to cut costs and maybe even make layoffs of their staff.

Of course, it could be that you are more likely to view things as favorable when you have a better current financial condition. I'm not suggesting these are cause and effect, that being optimistic leads to better finances or that your pessimism will be linked to never achieving wealth. It highlights that moods and outlook are associated with financial decisions and impact how you make choices.

CASE IN POINT

Ron was a 23-year-old recent graduate of a California university with a degree in engineering. He, fortunately, had the financial support of his parents, who paid for all of his school. He graduated with no debt and immediately was recruited by a Texas-based oil firm and offered a good salary. He was generally optimistic about his future and considered purchasing a home despite working only a few months. His mood and outlook shaped his decisions. Ron's friend Tom struggled through school and found himself with over $21,000 in student loan debt. He hasn't been able to find a job with the degree he earned. Tom's general outlook is more pessimistic and cautious, and he rented a small one-bedroom apartment. Mood and outlook alter both of their money management choices.

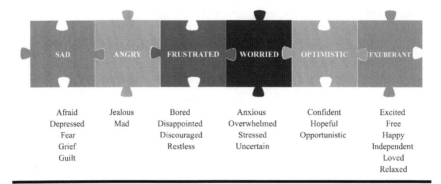

SAD	ANGRY	FRUSTRATED	WORRIED	OPTIMISTIC	EXUBERANT
Afraid	Jealous	Bored	Anxious	Confident	Excited
Depressed	Mad	Disappointed	Overwhelmed	Hopeful	Free
Fear		Discouraged	Stressed	Opportunistic	Happy
Grief		Restless	Uncertain		Independent
Guilt					Loved
					Relaxed

Figure 3.4   Range of Feelings.

Likewise, if you are in a great mood today, you might be more inclined to spend more (over-buy or over-spend) or take other types of actions than you might if you were in a bad mood. Think about that. Have you ever purchased something big when you were in a good mood? It's pervasive. Moods are more temporal and constantly changing and are influenced by events or triggers that are not necessarily long-lasting, like your emotions or personality traits. What one person does in a good mood might be what somebody else would do in a bad mood. So, there can be no generalization about a person in a good mood spending more money or making poorer choices. Notice for yourself how moods impact what you choose daily. Moods impact our choice processes and our financial health.

There is an extensive range of potential feelings and emotions, ranging from sadness and depression to exuberance and joy (Figure 3.4).

Each of these feelings has its unique impact on everyone's financial outlook and decision-making. Some feelings might cause you to short-cut the normal reasoning, while others might cause you to avoid making decisions altogether. All of these are essential emotions and ones we might experience multiple times per day even. We need to recognize them and attempt to re-frame our perspectives to make more balanced decisions when we do. The use of the financial decision journal shown earlier is really helpful for examining the effects on our own choices.

Table 3.1 summarizes some of the more common emotional patterns and their potential impact on finances.

External Influences on Choices

Not only do our brains sometimes work to sabotage our thinking, but other people and objects also intervene—we don't operate in a vacuum. Especially

Table 3.1   Behavioral Finance Impact of Emotions on Choices

Emotion or Mood	Behavioral Finance Impact
Anger	Quicker, more impulsive decisions. More reactive or brash. Anger is one of the most dominant of emotions that impact our choices.
Defensive	This causes you to take a posturing position. You are less likely to take feedback or recommendations and to negotiate less effectively.
Fear	Fear creates uncertainty and ambiguity, which might lead you to delay investing or hoard resources. Fear is one of the most dominant emotions impacting money management.
Guilt or shame	Guilt and shame create uncertainty, embarrassment, or even fear of taking any action. They tend to result in a lack of clarity and less assertiveness.
Happiness	Joy and happiness could lead to overconfidence. You might be more inclined to spend more or buy more than intended or take different risks.
Jealousy	With envy, you are less logical and take more rash decisions, and it could distort your risk tolerance.
Over-confidence, pride, or hubris	These all tend to overestimate your risk tolerance and underestimate the riskiness of investments—increases how you perceive your ability to control outcomes.
Pessimistic, cynical	Negative emotions tend not to avoid "long" positions (those in the future rather than today). Focused on the likelihood of negative financial consequences.
Sadness	Sadness typically causes avoidance behaviors—you tend to delay or postpone activities due to feelings of being overwhelmed.

with social media and the internet, people are constantly being barraged by judging and evaluating our choices. When young teens see all their friends posting expensive cars on their Instagram pages, those with older and less expensive cars could feel less than worthy or inferior. This might cause somebody to try to purchase a vehicle they couldn't afford. The unfortunate result is that we feel we need to make decisions that others would reflect positively on rather than necessarily what we could afford or need. We need to find a way to activate both hemispheres of the brain. You can do this through simple techniques, such as shaking your body, talking to yourself, deep breathing, or getting outside perspectives.

Mindful Practice 9   Activate both your emotional and analytical hemispheres before making a choice.

The most significant external influences on our financial choices are our family, friends, and co-workers. Those closest to us can use a *nudge* to gently and indirectly suggest alternatives that modify our attention and focus on a better choice without using penalties or coercion.[36] These can be simple changes to the environment that might influence our decision-making, such as replacing the typical loaf of white bread with a loaf of organic wheat bread. A nudge can be helpful, such as one partner pointing out to the other that they are smoking more than usual. But advertising and salespeople can also use nudges to alter us to buy more or differently. A nudge that encourages more expensive items than we could afford can result in loans and higher credit card balances than we needed. Your friend might say something like, "I think you look great in that dress." You are probably more likely to buy something when you hear that. Or your mom might say, "I don't think you should take that job." Small comments from those around us elicit significant emotional responses.

Even those outside our circle can influence decisions. Consider the impact that an excellent salesperson can have on your choices. Sales personnel training involves the art of *overcoming objections* (or negating your doubts) to price or features by appealing to your emotions—which we know is both easy to do and highly effective at de-railing decision processes. For instance, here are some of the more common objections that salespeople have used over the years to influence and change our buying and investing behaviors.

- "There are only one of those left. You better act fast."
- "Interest rates are about to go through the roof. Buy it today so you can lock in a good low-interest rate loan."

- "If you don't act now, prices will surge next week. My boss just told us about the price increase."
- "People are calling me nonstop to request showings of this real estate property. I have four other showings right after you, so if you're interested, you better move quickly."

Other people influence emotional decisions, so we must figure out how to minimize these external influences and rely on our information sensing and processing. It is virtually impossible to leave emotions and feelings out of decisions, so how do we incorporate them into sound financial decision-making processes?

> *To avoid sales pressure, assert yourself and set boundaries. Remember you are in control.*

Congruity: Balancing Our Emotions

Modern neuroscientists believe that our brains constantly integrate our moods, feelings, and emotions with our thoughts.[37] So how are we to make rational, well-thought-out financial choices? One solution is to align both sides of our brains—I call this activating behavioral congruity. We must find a way to harness these emotions, to use them in positive ways to influence our choices. The best way to do this is to understand how we balance our feelings with our reasoning. We should strive to contain our thoughts where they could skew our decisions. But we also need to lean on our emotions to improve our judgment and intuition. Emotions and cognition are not at odds with each other; they work together much like oil and vinegar. Easier said than done, but we will discuss some specific tips to make this happen (Figure 3.5).

What makes the most sense?
Cognitive reasoning
Analytical processing

What do I feel like doing?
Emotions
Senses
Feelings
Moods

Figure 3.5   Balancing Emotions and Cognition (Behavioral Congruity).

If we rely solely on our emotions, we might be more inclined to make impulsive decisions which we may or may not regret. Emotions can move through our brains much faster than rational thoughts. The quality of our decision (the outcome) is tough to judge because there is no way to compare if we would have made a different decision what the effect might have looked like. We could speculate, but we never know. But generally, impulsive decisions should be paired with some time for considering other alternatives. For example, suppose a parent told their daughter that buying something was a bad idea. In that case, the daughter could react to this either positively ("Okay, I accept your opinion") or negatively ("I will buy it anyway"). Either way, there is now an emotion, a feeling, or an affect attached to the purchase. The same thing happens with all kinds of personal financial situations, such as buying stocks based on our feelings or choosing a specific insurance company.

Companies know that our emotions drive our choices, which is why so many television commercials focus less on products and more on feelings. They target their ads to attach to our emotions, which could result in a purchasing or investing decision. Brands also elicit feelings. Brands such as Starbucks, Coca Cola, and even Marlboro cigarettes trigger certain feelings which can stimulate consumers to act in one way or another even though this is often at our subconscious level.

Activating Congruity

Before making that next choice, closely consider your emotions. Are you unusually stressed? Do you feel more sad or more excited than usual? Whatever the emotion, rest assured that it has some impact on your money choices. Think about the effect that this mood might have. Imagine a scale, shown in Figure 3.6, that you could use to measure how you're feeling. Now record this emotion and the numeric scale for all money choices you make.

The best way to capture this is in a financial decision journal—basically a notebook, phone app, or electronic journal. Many people journal their dreams, their concerns, or their day in general, but very few document about money! This is a huge mistake and opportunity. We can learn a lot about our rationales for decisions if we can look back over time and see what was happening. To make a journal really useful, we must consider each choice we made of any significance, as well as how we were feeling that day and why we made the choice that we did.

Think back at the end of every day on any significant decisions you made that day. You'll need to define what qualifies as substantial. For some of you, that might mean anything over $20. For others, it might be anything over $100. That is up to you, but these are choices that impact how you spend your free money and potentially alter how you can make other choices.

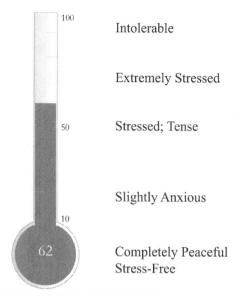

Figure 3.6   How Do I Feel Today?

Make a list that outlines the choice (what was it you did or decided?) and how you made it (e.g., by intuition or active thought)? Try to identify the number of seconds or minutes of contemplation or thought given to the decision. Be sure to make a note of how you are feeling at that time: happy, sad, bored, scared? Do this for a week. Put the journal by your bed or carry it with you in your purse or bag.

Mindful Practice 10   Incorporate a daily financial decision journal.

For instance, you chose to go to the grocery store. Did you actively choose which one to go to? Which route to drive? What you needed when you got there? If we can take a few seconds to bring awareness to this choice and explore the implications, we are much more likely to make better decisions. Try going back through your list every day and see what trends emerge in your own life. Use Table 3.2 to document your thoughts.

Table 3.2 Financial Decision Journal

Today's date/time:	_____
Decision I made (or intend to):	_____
$ amount involved:	_____
Why (goals for choice)?	_____
	_____
What are/were my choices?:	1._____
	2._____
	3._____
What are desired outcomes?	_____
How will I know if this is a successful decision?	_____
How am I feeling today?	_____

   □ Sad   □ Happy   □ Limited   □ Anxious

   □ Scared   □ Optimistic   □ Brave   □ Confident

   □ Other   _____

Emotional scale (0–100)   _____

How could I have done this differently?   _____

Decision-Making Strategies

Strong positive and negative emotions can cloud your judgment, causing you to spend, save, invest, or give differently than you might otherwise in a more neutral feeling or mood. But emotions also have a positive role in decision-making. They actually can help us, as well as hurt us. Our financial behaviors are influenced heavily by our mental health. Conversely, taking care of your mental health will lead to better financial behaviors. If you can catch yourself feeling these intense emotions, you are much less likely to be able to focus on money matters. That might not be the priority, so uncertainty, delays, and avoidance are all quite common. We also might become reactive. When this happens, you might make sub-par decisions on spending and investing.

Beyond the use of a financial journal, you need to work on improving your decision strategies. These are some strategies you can use to align your choices.

1. **Awareness.** Understand your dominant style. Do you consider yourself to be more emotional or analytical? Look at how you typically react to certain events before answering. You may not notice it at first, but you have a leaning one way or another. Find out which way and try to compensate by overtly activating the other side of your brain. This takes work, and your journal can help you recognize patterns.

2. **Triggers.** Identify what triggers your emotions, moods, and behaviors. Recognize how these behaviors impact you specifically. Note if any specific situations tend to activate one of the two sides of your brain more. See if you can isolate particular cases where you were pushed to do something you otherwise might not have done. Make a list and write these down in a journal.

3. **Breathing.** Incorporate long, deep breaths for at least 30 to 60 seconds before making any decisions. Research has shown that the simple act of breathing mindfully can activate changes in your nervous system, which reduces your heart rate and improves the ability to make decisions.[38] Let the new oxygen circulate and slow down your brain and heart so you can think clearly. Breathing is a crucial exercise in mindful money management.

4. **Reverse polarity.** Reversing polarity is recognizing and activating the non-dominant neural process. Basically, you attempt to do the opposite of what you would instinctually do for a certain period. If you are emotional, try to incorporate analytical thinking daily and vice versa. Force yourself to do something different even with non-financial choices. Use your left hand (if you are right-handed) or paint (if you are more analytical)—anything to activate different processes within your brain.

5. **System.** Create a central place within your home to store all bills, receipts, and files related to finances. Utilize a common approach to all money choices. Create a system of organization can help reduce uncertainty.

6. **Time matters.** Work on making financial decisions at a day and time when you feel the presence of less strong emotions. Dedicate a small portion of your day when your mood is neutral, you feel less anxious or stressed, and you can devote the time and energy to money choices.

7. **Relationships.** If you're married or have a partner, make sure both of you are in agreement and reach the same decisions. Emotions impact both people differently, and communication between spouses is important in creating less tension about decisions. Ensure that both partners have a clear financial picture of where you stand in terms of budget, expenses, assets, and liabilities. You need to be aligned on money matters.

8. **Obtain outside, independent advice.** Financial coaches and advisors that are independent can help bring clarity to decisions when you are uncertain or struggling emotionally, as can other accountability partners, colleagues, and friends.

Take Away

- Our brains are not necessarily rational and don't always search for the best financial decisions.
- Money management choices made on autopilot often mindful choices.
- Emotions impact our behaviors, and decisions are naturally shaped by judgment and intuition.
- The quality of our mental health further shapes our financial behaviors.
- Seek to bring awareness to all choices.
- Look for alignment or congruency between your analytical and emotional mind. Activate using several decision strategies, such as breathing, journals, reversing the polarity, and outside assistance.

Key Terms

analytical, autopilot, behavior, behavioral counterforce, behavioral economics, behavioral finance, bounded rationality, cognition, emotion, fallacy, judgment, neural network, nudge, overcoming objections, present bias, prospect theory, psychology, rational, reasoning, stereotype, utility

Chapter 4

Overcoming Fear and Uncertainty

"Human behavior flows from three main sources: desire, emotion, and knowledge."

Plato

Can you recall when you were 100% confident that you made the right decision, especially when your money was on the line? Most of us have a fair amount of doubt, uncertainty, and fear when making decisions that might cost us our hard-earned cash. This chapter describes how to overcome the dominant emotion that handicaps us in money—fear. Fear is the emotion that we will not have enough, that we made a wrong decision and don't want to take risks. Fear (and uncertainty due to chance) stops us from moving forward. To move through the steps of wealth, you must conquer fear!

Uncertainty: Fear of the Unknown

Certainty is the lack of risk or when we know things for sure. *Certainty* is the condition in which you are always correct, and you have no doubts. To always be right, you'd have to avoid activities with the highest returns. In essence, to be sure about an outcome, you would likely avoid nearly everything. A state that has complete certainty, and no randomness or chance, is called *deterministic*. This suggests that if you do something, you will always get the same result every

DOI: 10.4324/9781003231844-5

time. It is not realistic for personal choices, whereas a *stochastic* decision recognizes the randomness and uncertainty built into every aspect of our lives.

One of the core principles of money management is that we constantly deal with the unknown, with which we lack familiarity. Money management is stochastic. We all have a bias leaning towards that which we know and are comfortable. We enjoy a sense of nostalgia and familiarity and tend to suffer from an *ambiguity effect*, in which we subconsciously avoid unclear paths forward. So, for instance, driving down any new road is an unknown, as is investing in a stock when you have never done it before. If you have never put any money in a mutual fund, your natural tendency is never to invest and to keep the money in your savings. Scary horror movies are perfect for introducing unknowns that create fear. We must be mindful of this and consciously bring awareness to it so we can address it.

Fear can be good. *Fear* causes us to run from danger and to avoid certain risks. Fear will avert us from dangers and threats and help guide us towards safer, less-risky choices. But fear can also wreak havoc on your decision-making style. Fear of the unknown includes

> **Anxiety and uncertainty are both forms of fear.**

not knowing what to expect when you make a choice. If you knew what would happen under all conditions, this would be a state of certainty. Uncertainty is much more common. *Uncertainty* is the lack of something being known and familiar, which causes us to rely on our brain's ability to make guesses based on what could be likely to occur. This is usually the starting point for our decision failures. We really are not good at estimating potential outcomes in advance, no matter how good we think we are! This brings us to an important principle with regards to the brain. Uncertainty that is not confronted will lead to anxiety and fear, and fear is typically a significant reason we avoid specific actions. Uncertainty and anxiety are both types of fears.

Uncertainty is everywhere, and we must fight our instinct to wait for it to subside. But waiting for a state of complete certainty will nearly guarantee that returns will be minimal. On the other hand, we don't want to act too quickly and rush into decisions. Looking for a sweet spot between these two extremes is important.

Mindful Practice 11   Do not wait for complete certainty before making a choice.

With regards to our money choices, the key is to utilize tools to reduce the amount of uncertainty we are dealing with as we go through stages of wealth building. It's not practical or effective to just say "don't be afraid" or "don't fear the unknown." That doesn't work. But there are some small behavioral tips which you can use to reduce the anxiety that comes with uncertainty.

Take Healthy Levels of Risk

Risk helps to create the emotions of fear, anxiety, and worry. *Risk* is defined as the likelihood that something bad or negative will happen or that danger is lurking nearby. Sometimes our brains are protecting us. When we see people fighting in the streets with guns, our brains naturally seek to avoid that danger and will hopefully lead us elsewhere. For most people, if they see a burning building, they naturally run out of the building. However, we are very fortunate that some people have the opposite tendency and become firefighters and emergency medical technicians. But our brains also do the same thing with any potential danger or loss and seek to avoid negative consequences from all decisions and actions. We need to have a healthy respect for risk, but we must remember that everything in life involves some degree of risk, and we must learn how to navigate the risks, taking some and avoiding others.

If you want to make the largest gain or returns on your money in personal finance, you must take the largest risk. Modern portfolio theory has long established the risk–return relationship.[39,40] Those who gambled early on when a fledgling company named Amazon first started home deliveries of household items and bought the stock when it was released paid $18 per share. That was in 1997. For most people, that was extremely high given that the company had an unproven business model. The business could easily have failed, succeeded, or just kept the same share of the market. There was no real benchmark for that type of company, and early investors took a big risk if they invested in the stock. Today, in 2021, that same share of stock is nearly $3,600. That is a cumulative return of well over 200× your initial investment, or 25% per year! That is nearly impossible to fathom such a large return compared with current savings rates at banks of less than 1/10th of 1%.

Hundreds of thousands of businesses start every year. Many fail. How do we isolate the Amazons in an investment choice and not the others? This remains a big issue. Even with supercomputers, mathematical algorithms, and continuous monitoring, even experts pick poorly routinely.

There is a direct relationship between risk and return. Most of us don't want to take extreme risk or to lose it all. I love this quote from famous author T.S. Eliot. "Only those who will risk going too far can possibly find out how far one can go." In other words, we cannot predict who is taking excessive risks or going too far, but we do know some degree of risk is necessary to accumulate wealth. On the other hand, if we do want to have the best outcomes from our financial decisions, we will probably need to become comfortable with risks. Nearly everybody has benefitted from the long-term gains from riskier investments, such as stocks, mutual funds, and indexes. According to the author of one of the largest studies on millionaires every conducted (Thomas J. Stanley), nearly 80% of all millionaires are active investors and contribute at least 15% of their income to investing each year.[41]

When we fear making choices, we tend to avoid them. And when we avoid or fear them, we usually make poor money choices. We must take a reasonable and healthy degree of risk to get wealthy. We need to tackle our fears.

=====================================

Mindful Practice 12   Confront your financial fears.

=====================================

Check Your Vision

Risk is often only measured by perceptions, not reality. It may be a reflection on the slice of data you are exposed to, or your perspective. Consider this graph in Figure 4.1. Using data from the Dow Jones Industrial Average (DIJA), which is an average of stock price data from 30 of the largest companies in the world and serves as an index of performance in large companies, the change in average stock values are displayed over time. Despite some periodic declines, there is a dominant pattern of increase. From January 1992 through June 2021, a period of 355 months, the DJIA has averaged .74% monthly return (or nearly 9% annually).

If you had this vision or perspective early on, you probably would have invested in the DJIA and would have been doing really well. But what if you had a different lens, and you only had a very narrow vision on certain dates? Consider the identical results but during only a short time period such as during 2001 and 2002 (Figure 4.2)? What would your tendency towards risk be if these were the only data you had? Would you have made any investments? Would you have hoarded cash? What would you do?

Keep in mind that these two graphs show the same data. The only difference is the time period (our frame of reference, or lens) which we use to view them. Consider another example.

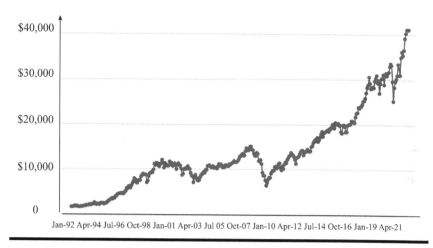

Figure 4.1   Historical Equity Returns, Long-Term Perspective.

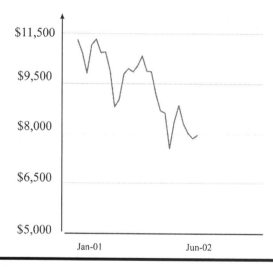

Figure 4.2   Historical Returns, Narrowed Lens.

CASE IN POINT

You are walking in a shopping mall and see a sign that says, "2 scoops, any flavor ice cream, 50% off for next hour only." You stand in a small line and save $2 and are quite pleased. But then you find out later they dropped the price to only 50¢

(you paid $2; the original price was $4). Now you are upset that you overpaid and could have had four times the amount of ice cream for what you paid. The lens or perspective which you frame the choice around if often dictated by the time frame which you are observing. But it doesn't change the fact that you still got a good deal and saved 50% originally. If you invest in a market that temporarily has price shifts, as all good markets do, you will be purchasing some things at their high, some at their low, and some in between. The key to making good choices is to make "most" near the low range but not all.

When we think of ourselves as more mindfully oriented, behavioral investors, we must gain a better vision. We must zoom out to a larger time frame (and zoom in when necessary) to get a more comprehensive point of view. Notice that the results would have been identical. The charts are identical. The only difference is the perspective. Keep in mind that the only people that would have lost any money during these two years are those who sold (or recognized) these losses during the downtimes. If you would have sold, you would have done so at the worst possible time.

Mindful Practice 13   Never sell assets during a down market!

Going back to the Dow Jones historical data, let's say you inherited $50,000 in 2000, which was a generally a period of recession, or decline in the economic output across the United States. Over the past 21 years, using the rate of return from the DJIA since that specific month (0.5% monthly, 6% annually), if you would have invested it in the index and left it there, your money would have grown to $175,000. That is a more than tripling of that money over that time period. While others might have immediately spent it, you chose to invest it and now have an additional $125,000 for the future.

If your perception of risk caused you to avoid investing this, and you

Ask yourself: am I using the right perspective here?

would have simply put that into a bank account (with the historical average since then averaging 0.09%), your ending balance would have grown to just at $51,000 over 21 years—a return of only $1,000 in over two decades.

There is little risk in putting money under your pillow or in a bank account. Bank savings, certificates of deposits, and savings bonds are typically called *risk-free rates* since they involve little risk and essentially provide little return. If you want to become wealthy, you probably should opt for some degree of risk.

Risk Profile Types

Although we want to know ourselves deeply, we often don't. We don't really know what we feel or what we would do unless we think it through. We don't often contemplate such deep thoughts on a daily basis, as we go about our normal routines. However, to become mindful and gain insight into our own brain with regards to risk, we must understand our risk types. On the continuum between risky and risk averse with regards to money, are you more likely to make aggressive choices or more conservative ones? Knowing yourself and your tendencies is important, as it brings to light your subconscious biases.

To try to better understand your own tolerance for risk, try answering these three questions shown in the Table 4.1. For a link to the full risk tolerance and money personality assessments, please see the supplemental materials available on the book website.

Risk Aversion

How we sense (perceive) risks, how we interpret risks directly and indirectly on our choices, and how we either avoid or attack these risks are central to our financial decision-making. There is risk in everything we do each day, including driving a car, walking on a sidewalk, or even walking in a grocery store. The way we perceive these risks and prioritize them in our minds shape how we act. If we are fearful of all risk and wish to avoid it, there will be consequences. In finance, risks are associated with greater returns. So, the more comfortable we are with understanding the risks and carefully balancing these when deciding, will have positive impact on our money management.

When we allow fear of risk to completely avoid certain activities, such as investing in the stock market because we are concerned about declines, we are

Table 4.1   Brief Risk Tolerance Assessment

1. Assume that you invested $10,000 today, and this was the only money you had outside of your cash reserves in savings, and the investment balance dropped to $1,000 next year. How would you respond?

   a. Avoid dealing with this issue.

   b. Sell all of the remaining balance, take your losses, and fire your financial advisor.

   c. Continue your current strategy and not change a thing.

2. Which of the following do you fit most closely with?

   a. I am more concerned with not losing any of my money than making any money.

   b. I prefer a guaranteed small return with minimal risk.

   c. I am more interested in how big the potential gain can be.

3. If you had a 10% chance to win $10,000 by only spending $1,000 today and a 90% chance of losing it all OR a guaranteed gain of $250 what would you prefer?

   a. Avoid taking any action.

   b. Take the definite gain of $250.

   c. Take the 10% probability of a $1,000 potential gain.

Scoring. Add up all the responses, assigning scores based on:

A = 1 point; B = 2 points; C = 3 points.

If you scored 3, you are extremely risk averse. Scores between 4 and 6 indicate moderate to low risk tolerance. Scores between 7 and 9 suggest you are more willing to take risks.

showing signs of risk aversion. *Risk aversion* can be defined as how consumers and investors prefer certainty over any uncertainty and alter their behaviors because of perceptions of risk.[42,43] People tend to be risk averse when they believe they have limited options and resources.

Risk aversion is closely related to the concept of loss aversion. *Loss aversion* is when a consumer is more likely to place greater weight on not losing any money rather than gaining any increase. For example, if you have a chance to gain or lose $100 by investing $20 and a $5 definite gain if you spend $1, a loss-averse consumer would rather take the $5 option because there is no potential for loss, and risks are significantly limited. The downside to risk and loss aversion, though, is that without some degree of risk, your expected future values are extremely limited.

Suppose you chose not to invest in equity mutual fund but instead kept all of your money in cash. In that case, you essentially prefer a risk-free level of return over the potential to earn significantly higher returns. A consumer willing to accept higher levels of risk in exchange for the opportunity to earn higher returns on investment will potentially yield a substantially greater wealth effect in the long run. The low-risk strategy may be useful in some periods, such as when the stock market is decline or bond yields decrease, but knowing when those periods exist is nearly impossible to predict. Avoiding all losses and risks for the guaranteed certainty of low returns is not a wise choice for building wealth.

Mindful Practice 14   Remember this:
99.9% of the time, a bad decision
will not destroy you.

Emotions and Affordability—Can You Afford it?

You should always ask yourself this question before you do something: can I really afford this? What I have noticed, though, is that the definition of the word "afford" is interpreted emotionally and used quite differently between people. Technically, *afford* means the ability to pay for something. So, for many folks, if you ask if they can afford something, they either can look at the balance in their checking account, and if the amount of the purchase is less than their available balance, believe they can afford it. Or, if it's a small enough, they assume they can afford it because they look at the monthly salary and believe it should be sufficient to cover it. The use of credit cards has worsened this problem because technically, anybody could "afford" to purchase nearly anything given a credit card or loan. This is one reason why the number and sizes of student loans and car loans have risen so dramatically. Colleges and vehicles that were once accessible only to a small few are now available to everybody—but at a huge cost.

To become wealthy, we must change the definition of that word in terms of how we apply it. Recall the formula for wealth accumulation: wealth = money saved and invested after we spend and give. So, money spent (whether on credit or with cash) depletes wealth. I propose that a better definition of the word *afford* could instead be is this the best use of my money? Affording something should not be interpreted as *can* it be bought, but *should* it be? The use of the financial decision journal shown earlier will be helpful because it forces you to think about your choices, why you made them, and whether they were considered successful.

For example, if you view that you can afford a new vehicle because you can make the monthly minimum payment, you are ignoring two key wealth-building concepts:

- *Opportunity cost.* The same money you spent for one purpose could have been used for something else.
- The power of *momentum*. Money used for savings and investments creates additional forward momentum through compounding and growth over time, which make any amount of money magnify in future years.

Always consider the opportunity cost and impact of momentum when making purchase decisions. We must re-train the way our brain thinks about money, affordability, and daily choices. Part of that involves getting comfortable with uncertainty.

Barriers to Developing Wealth

Overcoming the obstacles to building wealth requires you to recognize and avoid them. But some are more mundane, like our approach to money, while others require more thought required from the financial planning process. Some of these obstacles to wealth include:

- Fear, anxiety, and uncertainty. These emotions stop us from moving forward and taking decisive actions.
- Our own cognitive limitations and shortcuts. We all take mental shortcuts to simplify, speed up, and reduce the burden on our brains from time to time. Routine decisions that can be automated or made at the subconscious level take less brain power, but they also might not be well-conceived.
- Denial about their limitations and situation. Many of the people I've worked with who are in financial straits are in denial about their condition. Many people who could take advantage of Medicaid, food stamps,

and other assistance often do not believe they are "desperate" enough for these programs. Others who earn a high paycheck are often in extreme levels of debt, either due to credit or taxes, but are in denial about their condition.

- A lack of financial purpose or vision. If there is no sense of purpose in why you are savings, investing, and accumulating wealth, it becomes an obstacle to growth. Identifying a vision helps your brain align with your financial choices.

- Lack of the proper foundation in the money pyramid, specifically in emergency cash reserves and routine savings (described in Chapter 9). There is a preferred order for how to accumulate wealth. Maximizing retirement investing while you are in extreme credit card debt is an example of a poor timing. I will introduce the financial pyramid concept later.

- Inability to control our spending and lack of financial discipline. Our own lack of discipline in sticking with a plan, with routine monitoring of our choices, and being consistent is one of the most common barriers to wealth management.

- Lack of consistency. It sounds boring, but consistent decisions made over the long-run will usually out-perform sporadic and risky choices.

Dealing with Uncertainty

Uncertainty of all forms—risks, anxiety, fear—should be managed so they don't overwhelm you. The best way to do this is to identify the risks, analyze and quantify them, and then manage them. For example, let's assume you were afraid that if you invested money into the stock market, you would lose it all. We would start with trying to really understand the root of the fear. Is the risk really that you might lose it all? Or is the risk that you might lose some part of it? How probable is either condition? Start by trying to assign a realistic estimate for the likelihood of a loss (e.g., 25% reduction). What would be the total impact this might make on the total? What might be the upside, or the gain? You need to balance out the full impact of the risk—upside and the downside—and estimate the likelihood of either of these or some midpoint in between. Given what you know, are you willing to lose or gain that much? This is the most difficult part of confronting uncertainty. We can't predict the future.

We can estimate or partially predict based on the past, though. If we do research, we can look for patterns or changes over time and see how investments or prices are changing and performing. It might give us some insight, but it is not sufficient without the use of judgment and other inputs. Life is just too uncertain.

Decision Strategies for Confronting Uncertainty

Most of us will settle on a certain degree of risk. We don't always need a risk-free situation, but we also don't want to take a great amount of risk. In essence, we must find a sweet spot of risk that will yield a reasonable return for the amount of risk we want to talk. Any time that you face a decision involving money, consider employing all the following strategies.

1. Take stock of your situation. We are all guided by emotions and behaviors, often becoming "stuck" on one way of thinking, one perspective. Try to figure out your perspective, which you gravitate towards. Do you usually look for worst-case scenarios? Is a failure from previous years hampering how you think about opportunities? Do you tend to not research things thoroughly and make instinctual decisions? Whatever your tendency is, try to balance it out and take stock of the perspective.

2. Name your fears and concerns. What is it you are afraid of? What is holding you back?

3. Attempt to place real estimates on potential impact, and returns, this might have on your decision.

4. Bring this fear or risk out into the open. Talk about it openly. Confront it. Don't let it own you.

5. Use a daily decision journal to document how you feel during different times of day and decisions.

6. You are often thinking about specific potential outcomes—the fear you lose everything. We think in extremes. Try to quantify this risk more clearly and see how likely it really is.

7. Consider the impact of time. Separate other aspects of the choice (such as price or benefits you might receive) from the timing. Ask yourself "If this were two years later, would I do it then" or "If I wouldn't have known what just happened, would I make a different decision?." Sometimes the choice is dependent only on the timeframe you are looking at. For instance, you probably don't want to spend money for new windows on a house that was just destroyed by a fire. But what about investing in a company that just had a fire whose stock dropped because of it. What's the likelihood a business will return to full operations again? Ask yourself, "Will they likely re-emerge and be just as successful after a small setback?" If you can separate the impact of time, you will be able to gain comprehensive perspectives more accurately.

8. Look for counterpoints. People with different skills, experiences, ages, and vocations often have different perspectives and provide a useful counterpoint to your existing paradigm. So, use this to your advantage. If you

decide to do something (or not to do something), challenge yourself by asking somebody who might disagree with your choice. Ask them about their logic. Try to really learn from it and see if there are any valid points. Do you still hold the exact same beliefs after these conversations? This could be your spouse, your parent, your friends, or even a co-worker.

9. Reward yourself for addressing the fear. Recognize your achievements.

10. Confirm all assumptions. Before you make the choice, just re-confirm internally that you have made selections using the correct assumptions. Make sure you fully understand all terms and inputs that go into the decision.

11. Use a decision checklist. Before taking off, airline pilots always run through a checklist. You can follow their example by asking yourself these important questions:

   a. What will happen if I choose to do absolutely nothing? What will be the outcome?

   b. What would be the worst and best-case scenarios? What do I stand to gain or lose if I make a choice?

   c. What decision is best for me in the long run (not just today)?

   d. How will I feel about my choice a year from now?

Feel free to add anything else you need to your specific decision checklist. This will help to ensure that you have a complete perspective and you are ready to choose wisely.

Take Away

- Fear can cause us to procrastinate, delay, and avoid making decisions. It can stop us from moving, pursuing that new job, or investing.
- Risk and uncertainty tend to create feelings of extreme conservativism in some and extremism in others.
- Know your own tolerance and preference for risk.
- Use a decision checklist when making choices involving risk.
- Recognize and confront your fears to achieve wealth and to balance risks with potential returns.

Key Terms

afford, ambiguity effect, certainty, deterministic, fear, loss aversion, momentum, opportunity cost, risk, risk-free rate, risk aversion, stochastic, uncertainty

NAVIGATING THE STEPS TOWARDS WEALTH

In order to become a wealthy person, you must change your choices.

The foundation of our quest for wealth starts by getting **F**rustrated with your current path, **A**ccepting responsibility, **C**ommitting to making better choices, and then **E**xecuting. **FACE**. Through the following few chapters, we will discuss this as we begin to move towards wealth. In Part II, we turn from understanding financial decisions and how the brain impacts our thinking to "how" to address these issues. Chapter 5 discusses how to find motivation for the changes. Chapter 6 discusses how to make detailed mindful money moves. Chapter 7 describes how to get rid of negative financial habits. In Chapter 8, we are specific about quantifying our financial goals. Chapter 9 explains maintaining the positive economic momentum necessary to cross our quest's second significant threshold (or bridge). We will walk through the Mindful Money Management Model and discuss how to avoid the biases and typical choice patterns that exist in each step.

DOI: 10.4324/9781003231844-6

Chapter 5

Step 1 — Get Motivated

"An investment in knowledge pays the best interest."

Benjamin Franklin

How did you get here, you might ask yourself? How did you get to a place of too much debt, payments you can't afford, or a lot less income than you expected? You wanted to be rich; now what? In step 0, you are stuck and barely getting by. But Part I laid the foundation for understanding the relationship between financial decision-making and the brain. You will need this as we turn now to address the barriers and biases that prevent us from moving through stages of wealth. In this chapter, we focus on how to begin to navigate through the mindful money model. We are at Step 1, getting motivated.

The Quest

Our quest starts by moving from getting by to getting motivated. In each of the following chapters, we will describe each of the steps to getting wealthy, including:

- Get by (step 0)
- Get motivated (step 1)
- Get mindful (step 2)
- Get rid (step 3)
- Get focused (step 4)

DOI: 10.4324/9781003231844-7

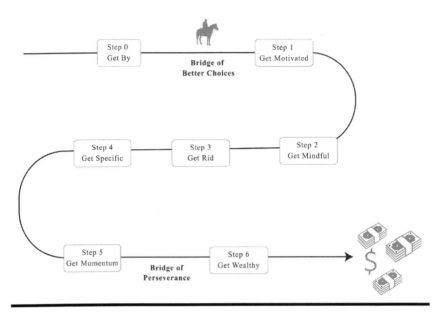

Figure 5.1   Quest for Wealth.

- Get momentum (step 5)
- Get wealthy (step 6)

Figure 5.1 reminds us of the mindful money roadmap.

Getting By

Many of you might currently be in this phase or remember a time when you once were. At this stage, you are barely making financial ends meet. In fact, it is estimated that 78% of all Americans are just scraping, or getting, by.[44] In this stage, you tend to fret and feel anxious about your finances. You are employed and receive an income, but it doesn't seem to cover all your expenses, and you are living paycheck to paycheck. The money mindset tends to be focused on *scarcity*, or a lack of resources. When you are trapped in this stage, there is an overarching concern about never having "enough," whether it's not enough salary or too little savings. This results in a philosophy of *avoidance*—you avoid the challenging aspect of dealing with your finances and plans because of either uncertainty, fear, or other negative emotions attached to finance. Procrastination about tough decisions is quite common. Some of you might recognize this in yourself—a feeling of dread when thinking about finances, either because they are too over-whelming, seem complicated, or just not at the top of your priority list.

People in this stage tend to be *reactive* as well. When you're reactive, you are transactional in nature and rely on quick judgmental responses rather than rational thought. If you respond with something immediately when it happens, rather than contemplating the best course of action before making a move, you are less likely to ponder the consequences and alternatives. If you think about this in terms of chess, it would be a player who takes a bishop only to find out that it exposed his own queen. Because of the scarcity of resources, there is a relatively high debt-to-asset ratio, meaning there are usually more liabilities (from credit cards and loans) then there are savings, investments, and assets. It is very important to practice separating an event from your reaction to bring awareness to it and allow time for contemplation.

Debt is an important consideration for moving through the stages of wealth. *Debts* are financial obligations that are owed to somebody else. Mortgages, car loans, and credit cards are the most common examples of debt. Debts reduce your wealth, as they are future obligations to spend your financial resources. There are many theories of debt—some suggest that you should employ debt as *leverage* (which helps to maximize your purchasing power). For example, you use a mortgage often to buy a larger home than you could otherwise afford if you had to save the entire cost upfront. Others consider debt to be what it is: a four-letter word! In this stage, however, you probably rely on debt and credit much more than you should.

> **Assess the role of debt in your financial strategy.**

When you're getting by, the method of record-keeping for your expenses is probably lacking. Either there is no system of keeping track of what you paid, or you use electronic payments but rely on your bank account for all records. There is no account reconciliation to ensure that what the bank paid is correct. Obviously, online bill payment can be more efficient and timely, but it doesn't always allow for aggregation and analysis. On the other hand, some clients prefer a check "register" and write down all expenses but don't use it in any systematic way to improve decision-making. This is problematic because errors do occur but mainly because you can't be proactive and plan when you don't have an organized system for tracking expenses through a budget.

People barely getting by often feel they have no choices—they get paid, and they pay bills. They feel they have no opportunities to save, invest, or do things differently. They might even feel the world has limited potential for them or it's acting against them. When you live paycheck to paycheck, it does not feel like you can get ahead, which further impacts your emotional state.

One particularly strong behavioral bias for people in this stage is that of the *status quo bias*. Here people tend to become comfortable with where they are and how it is working. You might enjoy this status quo and therefore do not take adequate steps to change your financial condition. Another strong bias is the *present bias* and *procrastination bias*, in which your brain places greater reward on the present moment rather than on the possibility of future rewards. Procrastination and delay are common, since fear and uncertainty tend to be dominant emotions in this stage.

Mindful Practice 15   Consciously resist the temptation to procrastinate.

Do you find yourself in this stage? Do the majority of what I describe sound like you? If so, keep reading for how to move forward. Get frustrated and fed up!

Frustration

As you are learning, developing wealth is partially physical or tangible, but it is predominantly mental. If we want to become wealthy, we must think like a wealthy person. What makes somebody financially poor versus rich is not that one is overly lazy and the other overly productive. Sure, hard work plays a definite role, but it's more than that. Luck, genetics, and education all are instrumental, but in fact, it has much more to do with the psychology or the mindset of those who become wealthy and differences in their decision-making style. What seems trivial, like being consistent or proactive, are traits that are cultivated and help us tame our emotions and fear. Getting out of dire financial straits requires you to get upset with this, to get frustrated.

You can work hard all your life and still barely get by. Does this make you frustrated? Are you angry that you don't have the resources you wanted? This is the first essential element: frustration. If you aren't frustrated with your situation, you won't have the motivation you need to make it through this quest. Frustration is the first element required to **FACE** your fears. **Frustration, Acceptance, Commitment, and Execution.** We must develop these four elements if we are to be successful in this quest. Figure 5.2 presents the FACE framework.

Acceptance

We need to start our journey here on step 1, reciting this word: acceptance. "I accept the financial condition which I am in." Don't deny it or constantly

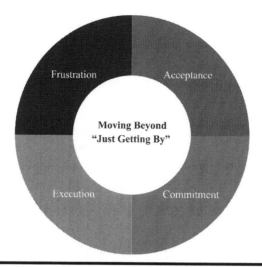

Figure 5.2   FACE Your Fears.

dwell on it. Don't worry about what caused your debt, who is to blame, why it happened. Just accept it. Accept it and take ownership for the situation. We ultimately are accountable for our own financial success. Many times, I've seen people deny they are in a certain situation and make comments such as "It was the college's fault that I took all those student loans." Accept that you are not where you want to be. Denial keeps us in the past. When we accept something as it is, we can then move forward.

Commitment

Commitment is defined as a condition of being obligated or emotion-ally beholden.[45] If we are obligated to do something, we follow through. Commitment is mental devotion to something. Have you resolved yourself to change? Commit to this fully by announcing it to your friends and colleagues. Positive intentions help to build lasting change.

Mindful Practice 16   Verbally and mentally commit to changes.

Commitment requires you gain the skills and knowledge necessary to manage money wisely. *Financial literacy* is the knowledge required to make informed judgments and to take effective decisions regarding the use and management of money.[46] When we are financially literate, we are aware of and educated about the investment and saving options, our spending behaviors, and are competent enough to perform the tasks necessary in money management.

Think about how famous athletes, whether they are golfers, tennis players, or basketball players, work on their weaknesses. They observe themselves closely, but they find role models who they can learn from. They see what others are doing, how they are hitting the ball, how they hold the racket, and what they are doing to become successful. In business, we call this *benchmarking*, in which we evaluate our own performance based on observing others performance; in effect, we are comparing ourselves against the standard or the best. The only way to do this is to gain financial literacy and knowledge. Choose to be curious about your finances and money in general. Set a goal of only 5 to 10 minutes initially per day to read a financial newspaper or magazine. Build on this over time until you feel you are financially knowledgeable in all areas.

Mindful Practice 17   Choose financial curiosity. Read, watch, and learn about finance daily.

Financial research has shown that there is a positive relationship between wealth and financial literacy.[47] There is a large payoff in long-term wealth accumulation for improving literacy across communities when controlling for other factors.[48] This suggests that we not only become financially literate ourselves but that we also educate our children, schools, parents, and others in our communities to become more financially literate.

Frustration, acceptance, commitment, and execution create lasting change.

Becoming financially literate also entails having an awareness of our gaps and what we alone cannot competently handle. For some, that might be collaborating with an investment advisor for retirement savings or with an insurance agent to get the best approach to managing auto and personal risks. We need to shore up any gaps in our literacy with independent collaboration and expertise from professionals that we trust.

We gain financial literacy through two simple methods: we take in more information about the topics we want to become more aware of, and we practice these skills! Good ways to learn more include watching YouTube videos from trusted sources, listening to podcasts, and reading financially oriented books and magazines. Watch your sources of information, though. Are they valid? Do they know what they are talking about? Are they themselves experts in their field?

Then practice these skills. Practice saving more than you did last month. Practice your spending skills by watching expenses each month. Practice and training are the keys to improving financial awareness and literacy.

Daily intentions which you could adopt such as "I will become wealthy," "I will get back on my financial feet.," or "I am financially mindful" are useful for change.

Mindful Practice 18   Practice daily intentions.

EXECUTION: GET MOTIVATED

Once we are fed up, we are more likely to change, but there is one important component that must be there—motivation. We must get the motivation to change and not just the willingness or ambition to change. We need the drive, the energy, the ambition, and the action. We must be ready, willing, and able to make the changes necessary if we are to move beyond stage 1 (getting by).

Motivation is described as the energy or drive that sustains individuals as we pursue changes in behaviors and pursuit of goals. More simply, motivation is why we do what we do. It explains why we pursue certain goals in life, what sports we play, what values we hold dear, and what we eat, for example. It explains quite a bit about who will achieve certain milestones in life and who will not.

Motivation explains why some people only dream about starting a new business or new job and others go out and get it. Motivation is largely derived from our ambitions in life. Most important, motivation is our brain's attempt to influence our body to act.

There are two major types of motivation: extrinsic (or external to oneself) and intrinsic (internal). We might be motivated to change if we were forced to declare *bankruptcy* or if a court rules we had to give up assets (examples of extrinsic factors). Bankruptcy is a legal action in which a court determines that somebody is unable to pay for outstanding debt and determines an appropriate course of action. Much more important to change, however, is the intrinsic perspective, which is when we internalize the need for change and begin to become willing to accept it. We can gain motivation by being fed up and having the willingness to change. Then we need to be ready, which suggests that we have made the change a top priority. Being able would imply that we have the toolset (the financial knowledge and capabilities) to begin the journey.

Ask yourself these questions:

- Am I really ready for changing my financial future?
- Can I commit to making this my top priority?
- Will I do what is necessary to make this financial evolution happen?
- Do I have the knowledge and tools necessary to get started?

If you answered "yes" to all of these, then you are ready to move to stage 2! Otherwise, work on why you didn't. If you're unhappy with the financial health, but you're not motivated, you'll need to fill in the gaps and work on that which you don't yet have in place. Here are some suggestions to keep you moving forward out of this stage.

Financial Strategies in This Stage

Your first financial move is to begin savings in an *emergency reserve*. This is money specifically set aside for potential emergencies—rare but costly expenses. Think about this as a contingency fund. All of your normal daily expenses need to be managed through your existing checking account, not this reserve. This reserve has one goal—to accumulate over time.

Be sure that you have opened a bank account at any bank or credit union which has reasonable interest rates, but more important, has a low fee structure. We will talk about fees in Chapter 7 in more detail. Compare a variety of options in your area at bankrate.com. You should open a savings or a money market account, which you will use to maintain your emergency reserves. This assumes you already have a checking account; if not, open that at the same time. A money market account pays like a savings account, except it pays slightly higher rates of interest. Every little bit counts at this stage.

Accounts can be opened online. When you go to do this, you will notice there is a minimum amount you must put in to open the account. Also, pay attention to the fee disclosures, which describes the types of monthly and transaction fees you could be charged. Fees can add up quickly—automated teller machine (ATM) withdrawals, insufficient funds fees, wire transfer fees, and others. The biggest one for you will likely be monthly services fees, which can range from $5 to $15 per month at different institutions. Be mindful of the fine print that says, "how to avoid this fee." Typically, setting up a paycheck direct deposit or making automatic deposits routinely will allow you to avoid this fee.

Weekly, add in a minimum fixed amount. At this point, even $25 or $50 per week would be good. We will go through how to streamline your budget soon, but you need to start changing your mindset by changing your practices. Practice not relying on this money. Forget that it is there and use your checking account for daily purchases; only use the reserve for deposits unless there is a true emergency.

Be mindful of all fees. Be mindful that you are focused on accumulating money in this account, so do not use or withdraw these funds! This is the beginning of your emergency reserve account (Table 5.1).

Table 5.1 Fundamental Financial Moves in Step 1

Activity	Date
Open money market account.	Today
Deposit a minimum of $25.	Today
Make weekly deposits of as much as you can afford.	Weekly
Monitor and dispute transaction statements.	Monthly
Automatic direct deposit of employer paycheck.	Each pay schedule

Daily Mantras

I have found words of encouragement during this step to be particularly helpful. You might find them useful as well, because they remind you of your strengths and the quest you are on. Daily you might consider using words of affirmation to help you move on, such as

> *I am on a journey to becoming wealthy.*
> *I have a healthy mindset.*
> *I am striving toward my goals.*
> *I accept responsibility for my current situation and am getting better every day.*
> *I make wise financial choices.*

I am convinced that once you develop your mindset to move out of this stage, you will be much better positioned to make the difficult choices that lie ahead.

Strategies for Changing Your Money Mindset

It is important to note that many people will eventually get out of this stage, but not all. It is quite possible that if you are not able to work through the behaviors that cause this stage to persist, you could end up remaining on a paycheck-to-paycheck basis your entire lift. Creating a mindset that is ready to go from thinking about "I have no money" to "I can do anything" is only possible if we move through the steps towards wealth. And the biggest hurdle is convincing our brains to get on board. Figure 5.3 shows some of the major changes we must make in our thinking during this evolution.

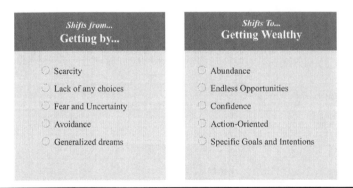

Shifts from... **Getting by...**	*Shifts To...* **Getting Wealthy**
Scarcity	Abundance
Lack of any choices	Endless Opportunities
Fear and Uncertainty	Confidence
Avoidance	Action-Oriented
Generalized dreams	Specific Goals and Intentions

Figure 5.3 Shift Your Money Mindset.

Financial progress requires a pattern of small decisions. Every decision you make forms a pattern. There could be one big decision that would put you in a much better place, such as selling your car and not having a $500 per month car payment, but more realistically, it will be a series of small steps forward. Try to think both incrementally (small money-savings tips) and sudden transformation (major changes that help transform your finances). Be creative and consistent. The question is how long are you destined to stay in this step?

The way to get beyond this step, try the following strategies.

1. **Stay positive.** This can be hard, but you must remain positive and optimistic during financial change. Avoiding the *negativity bias*, which is our natural tendency to focus on negative rather than positive thoughts and memories, will help you stay on track. How do you that? It's not easy, but every time a negative thought comes into your head, such as "I can't do this" or "I will never be wealthy," replace it with a different, positive thought. "I can do this" or "I will be wealthy soon." Don't let the negative financial thoughts stay in your head long and don't ruminate over them.

2. **Strive for emotional awareness.** This journey towards wealth begins by becoming mindful and conscious of where we are at and where we want to be. So, the first step to fixing a problem is to recognize it. Make each choice you make only after you have taken stock of your emotional well-being. How am I feeling right now? What mood am I in? Will this impact my decision tomorrow? Emotional awareness requires you to consider the effects that your behavior is having on your finances. Separating an action from your reaction is important; give yourself time to contemplate all small choices before your unconscious brain decides for you. You will learn more about this step in the next chapter.

3. **Build a bias for "action."** When you become frustrated with the lack of financial progress, you are inclined to build a bias towards action (rather than inaction). Choose to take an action over no action if you are stuck in stage 1. Build your emergency reserve account today. Don't dwell on the past and wallow in "what if." Just start doing something. Get active. When you are trying to make a change, it is important to do something, to take a positive action going forward with your finances. This can be a simple as thinking about your daily expenses, listening to a podcast about finance, or looking at the stock market daily summaries.

4. **FACE your fears**. You will need to be highly motivated to move beyond the status quo. Get excited about the journey to come. FACE your fears (get frustrated, accept your condition, commit to change, and execute). In physics and science, the inertia of gravity holds many objects back from forward momentum. The same is true in finance. *Financial inertia* is the

Table 5.2 Step 1 Summary

Summary	Get By
Overall financial profile	Struggling to make ends meet; living paycheck to paycheck
Money mindset	Scarcity and fear
Decision style	Reactive and avoidance
Key strategies	FACE, motivation, open money market accounts for emergency reserves
Financial system	Start with daily mantras
Current behavioral bias	Present, procrastination, status quo

persistence of stability and inaction and is largely associated with the status quo bias.[49] Inertia is what holds us down and does not allow us to evolve. Strong motivation (ready, willing, and able) for change is necessary to break the inertia.

5. **Focus on finance**. You should ideally be spending at least 5–10 minutes per day, for the first few weeks, on your finances. Spend it wisely listening to good podcasts, reading the financial section of your newspaper, or looking at factually based sources (such as Forbes, Wall Street Journal, Money. com, and other resources listed in Appendix B). Look at what is happening with stock markets by scanning if the market is going up or down in the previous few days. These actions will help you in learning the vocabulary of finance.

Table 5.2 summarizes each of the major points outlined in this chapter. We will build on this for each stage in subsequent chapters.

Take Away

- To move past getting by, we must become tired of our current situation. We must become frustrated (fed up!) with not having any savings, investments, or retirement savings and just living paycheck to paycheck.
- Motivation is ready, willing, and able to commit and follow through on actions.
- Change your thoughts to change your actions.

- Use daily mantras to help shift your mindset.
- Daily choose to become more financially knowledgeable.

Key Terms

benchmarking, emergency reserve, financial literacy, FACE, financial inertia, momentum, negativity bias, present bias, procrastination bias, reactive, scarcity, status quo bias

Chapter 6

Step 2 — Get Mindful

"Vulnerability is not weakness. And that myth is profoundly dangerous."

Brene Brown

Now that we have gotten motivated, accepted our quest, and committed to ongoing literacy and discipline, we are ready to adopt the wealth mindset needed to overcome financial inertia. The second step is where you have had enough of the status quo and begin to pivot towards more mindful money behaviors. This chapter aims to describe the steps necessary to become conscious and aware of your daily financial choices.

Awareness

You need to get mindful and plugged in. Mindfulness implies awareness and consciousness of your feelings and mind in the present moment.[50] If you think about it, you might still have the same attitudes and behaviors towards your finances as when you were just a kid. Most of us don't get good courses on money in school, and unless you are really interested in the topic, you only learn by doing and by observing your parents. Since you are at this step, you should celebrate the small behavioral "win" that you are aware of your situation and prepared to take action. This is the critical first step. Rewarding yourself for small wins are key to helping you to take continued action.

DOI: 10.4324/9781003231844-8

Mindful Practice 19   Mindful change = Self-awareness + Motivation + Action.

I really like the Brene Brown quote earlier about vulnerability.[51] Being *vulnerable* means you have exposed yourself and are open. With regards to finances, many people are not vulnerable. They insist that they have all the information they need or that they don't need help or assistance. They are not only stubborn, but they are also endangering their future because of their inability to be vulnerable. That's why in stage 2, we must get plugged in.

Mindfulness

So how do we raise our level of awareness so that we can move on to becoming more focused and financially fit? The brain plays an important part here. Awareness, or *consciousness*, has also been defined as the state of understanding and realizing something.[52] When we realize something, especially when it's different than our current thinking, we are encouraged (and even forced at times) to contemplate this difference.

Mindfulness focuses on raising our consciousness, paying attention in the moment, and drawing purpose from our behaviors.[53] Being mindful is an attempt to reduce that constant stream of thoughts running through our heads, many of which are negative. Mindfulness keeps us grounded in the moment so we are fully aware when we're buying that new suit or negotiating with a salesman. Even if it's for a brief period, we stop and think about the new perspective and our own thoughts. Sometimes we simply crystallize and fortify our own opinions and perspectives. Other times, we become a little enlightened, and we learned something new or appreciate a different perspective.

Wait, didn't I say earlier not to be focused on the present moment and to think more about the future? Yes, that is correct. We become mindful of the present moment but focus our time horizon on the decision impact for today and the future. When we are reflecting and learning about ourselves, it takes time and awareness focused on the present. Then, after reflecting, as we are going through the process of spending and investing money, think of both the present and the future.

We must leave time and space for bringing awareness to situations. If you go on with your daily routine without awareness, you will have the exact same results. Try to take away a new perspective and not simply reinforce your own perspective. That didn't work for you. You need something new. Once you realize it, you are more likely to take action.

One simple way to do this is to take a deep breath and spend a few seconds before any financial choice. Be mindful and aware of the impact of your choice before moving ahead.

Know Your Money Type

To be mindful, we must know ourselves and our money type. Each of us is unique, so there is no one magic ingredient or solution to our own path to wealth. If we are emotionally averse to taking risks, it is generally not a good idea to do that on an extreme level. We would want to consider risk in moderation, possibly. We can be inclined to be more than one of the four financial decision types. For instance, you can be more of spender or more of a saver, or you are so generous you give away all your money to charitable causes. Or you may be extreme in some categories, such as a hoarder (i.e., somebody who collects or accumulates more than they need). One of the keys to being mindful and conscious is to know our money types and make money decisions that reflect our own personality. Some basic money profiling types have been widely used to examine these different types.

I have developed an instrument that is grounded in my approach to behavioral money management to help you become more mindful about your style or approach to money management.

There are three primary factors in this model: risk, time horizon, and decision style.

Risk

What degree of risk are you comfortable taking? Do you tend to make decisions that are more conservative (less potential downside) or more aggressive (focused on maximizing returns)?

Time Horizon

What is your primary focus in building wealth? Is it a short-term goal or a long-term planning horizon?

Decision Style

What is your primary type of decision-making style? Do you tend to make decisions that are more spontaneous and emotional, or do you weigh your risks and benefits more analytically (Table 6.1)?

Table 6.1 Money Type

Factor	Ranging from	To
Risk	Conservative	Aggressive
Time horizon	Short term	Long term
Decision style	Impulsive	Analytical

There is a full instrument I developed for you to use and score online at my website yellowstone-consulting.com. Based on responses to the questions in each domain, you will fall within a range of the categories. There are six predominant money types based on combinations of which way you tend to lean in each area. Each type has an animal to help you associate your profile with their primary characteristics:

■ Crocodiles are fairly aggressive, more oriented towards the short term, and are more impulsive.
■ Turtles are generally conservative, focused on the long term, and are analytical.
■ Rabbits are conservative but focus on the long term and are more impulsive.
■ Cheetahs are aggressive and short-term oriented but analytical.
■ Mules are more conservative, short term, and impulsive.
■ Hyenas are aggressive, long term oriented, and analytical.

Table 6.2 presents these characteristics by money type.

It is important to know your money type. Which personality type do you think you have? None of these types is inherently good or bad. However, knowing where you fall on the spectrum provides insight into where you might make different choices as you move along your path towards wealth. If you are naturally more conservative, you might make daily reminders to take more risks or be a little more aggressive in some investments to balance out the more conservative ones. If you are too aggressive in taking risks, you will need tools to slow you down, to make you think more about risks, and to become more conservative.

Creating a Mindful Financial System

One task to becoming mindful is to create a system (or process) for organization. By system, I don't necessarily mean an information or electronic system; it could just as well be paper based. But a financial organization system implies that you

Table 6.2 Dominant Money Typology

	Type	Crocodile	Turtle	Rabbit	Cheetah	Mule	Hyena
Risk	Conservative		√	√		√	
	Aggressive	√			√		√
Horizon	Long term		√	√			√
	Short term	√			√	√	
Style	Impulsive	√		√		√	
	Analytical		√		√		√

have a regular and routine process for handing all of your financial transactions. It involves both how you approach the choice and how you record it.

I can find my car in the parking garage at work every time I leave—if I park on the same floor and in the same basic spot. If for some reason I change it up and park on the fifth floor instead of the third, my body might automatically return to three. When I get there and can't find my car, then I might remember that I parked on a different floor. Did I brush my teeth this morning? Did I shut the garage door? We do this in many aspects of our life, basically sleepwalking through our choices. This is a lack of mindfulness. A mindful approach to parking my car each morning is to consciously notice and remember images I saw as I parked my car and to record that information.

Approach

A *decision approach* is how you mentally prepare for an interaction involving any money choice. Think about how an athlete gets their "game face" on and prepares before a big game. They don't just stumble into the stadium or the arena. You must work on building yourself up before something big. Each time you have an opportunity to interact with a money choice, make sure you are in the right mindset. This could be before meeting with an advisor, before moving money into an investment, before paying your bills, or before negotiating with a salesperson. Avoid approaching issues when you are tired or anxious or have any extreme emotions. You want to be as mindful as possible. Then ask yourself a set of questions:

> *Is this the right thing to do?*
> *Is this the best price?*

Have I considered enough options?
Are there better choices for me?
Does this move me towards my financial goals?
What else should I know?

Think of the checklist we discussed earlier. If you know that you are about to purchase a car, prepare your approach. Set limits on what you are willing to pay, what terms you want, and what features you are willing to forego. Write down the important questions you want to have answered. Have your method of payment already lined up and ready. Get pre-qualified for a loan in advance, research the best rates, and then walk into the dealership. You must create a standard approach to all money choices before the situation arises.

System

Consider maintaining a physical storage and work area within your home for managing your invoices, bills, credit card statements, receipts, and important paperwork. Think about a distraction-free environment where you can focus; if you have an office, that is great. If not, find a place within your kitchen or living room where you can safely maintain files. You should have some form of separating "current" bills from "paid" ones. When you receive statements, think of breaking down money into categories like food or credit cards. I prefer to use physical folders over just electronic ones, as I feel it is more tactile and real in some sense. You can choose to do everything electronically, but it is essential to maintain a categorization system. I suggest developing a color-coded or labeled scheme for these papers. Also, rather than simply paying your bills as they arrive, try to actively manage them—setting up a control system, planning for balances, and becoming generally more proactive around daily money management. You will need to keep a ledger or tracking method for expenditures, savings, and investments. A simple ledger that shows who you are paying (or have paid), what it is for when it's due, is enough for now. In Chapter 8, I provide more extensive templates.

Some of you might ask: Now, why can't I just rely on what the bank sends me? Well, banks make mistakes, and systems are not programmed in our favor. The *automation bias* is our tendency to rely on electronic systems as our primary means of truth, when in fact we might make a completely different and better decision had we manually intervened. In addition, if everything is electronic, you make assumptions that it is handled appropriately and do not give it the same mindful attention. You need to get involved and work with your finances to get through the stages of wealth. Avoid the automation bias by keeping track of your receipts, bills, transactions, and statements.

Changing Behaviors

As you become enlightened about your lack of progress financially, you should prepare to change your behaviors, as we showed earlier in Figure 5.3. More than likely, you will consider several of the following behaviors:

- Spend less money than you are currently.
- Look for all opportunities to make a little more money.
- Identify ways to trim your expenses.
- Set money aside for long-term investments.

Change is difficult because it impacts your identity (who you believe you are, your purpose) and your beliefs (things you hold sacred). To make financial changes, we often have to re-imagine our vision for our financial self.

Mindful Practice 20   Re-imagine your financial identity and beliefs.

Avoid Common Behavioral Biases

Behavioral biases that are still at work in this phase include the automation bias (described earlier), *availability* bias and *anchoring*. The availability bias is at play because choices are typically made from within a limited range, from what is narrowly known or available to us.[54] At this point, you may not be relying on outside financial advice, so the availability of investing your money is limited. If you grew up in a family that did not invest, you probably don't know a good deal about investing. If your parents did not teach you about savings or have a savings account, you probably will not place a lot of weight on that because you did not have much exposure or emphasis on saving. Once we gain awareness of options and realize they are achievable, we are more likely to become motivated and stretch towards new goals.

Another common bias as mentioned is anchoring. *Anchoring bias* is when we rely on the first piece of information we hear or learn about and center our focus and perspective around that information. Anchoring tends to cause us to stick with certain investments because they were recommended to us or not buy or sell because the price is different from what you initially centered your mind around. For example, jewelry stores easily anchor your thinking about the amount of money to spend on a diamond engagement ring with statements such as, "You should plan on spending one to two times your monthly salary on an engagement ring." Then, when you get to the store, you might be pleasantly surprised to see the cost of a ring is only one month's salary rather than two. Or, if they suggest a ring for $12,000 and that is three times your monthly salary, you might be anchored now to the lower range. Car dealers can easily anchor us to a price using the sticker on the window. The fact is this sticker price may have no bearing on costs or what price the dealer is prepared to accept for the vehicle. Anchoring is a heuristic, or a shortcut, and it often limits and frames our thinking in negative ways.

If we grew up and our parents never discussed retirement savings or the concept of retiring at all, guess what? We are anchored to that same kind of thought pattern. Availability and anchoring bias are two of the major behavioral traps we must avoid.

Financial Strategies for This Stage

We should be making routine deposits into our emergency reserve fund at this step. All deposits are automatically performed through direct deposit established with your employer. Here we need to establish an initial investment account. Appendix B provides a list of some of the largest investment institutions—names such as Fidelity, Vanguard, and Charles Schwab. There are also specialized investment applications which are becoming more common, such as Robinhood or Webull. Do your research on their sites and pick one firm you like.

If you already have experience investing or with any specific firm, use that one. These are characteristics I watch out for when establishing an investment account:

- Required initial minimum investment
- Commission or trading fees for buying and selling investments
- Ongoing brokerage fees
- Monthly account fees
- Trading turnover ratio
- Total expense ratio
- Whether accounts are self-directed or sold by an investment advisor
- The breadth of funds and investments offered

At this step of wealth, you should be avoiding monthly fees of all sorts, so that those funds can be allocated into emergency reserves or investments. You may want to consider using an advisor to help you, or you can use one of the online tools at the site to help you conduct research.

Table 6.3 Largest Mutual Funds, Based on Net Asset Value, 2021[55]

Fund Name	Symbol
Vanguard 500 Index Fund	VFIAX
SPDR S&P 500 Index	SPY
Fidelity 500 Index	FXAIX
Vanguard Total Stock Market Index	VTSAX
iShares Core S&P 500 ETF	IVV

First things first: open an account online. Next, you need to choose the specific investment. If this is your first investment, a well-diversified, large-capitalization mutual fund might be a safe option. Given this is a portfolio of funds, most large firms are generally more stable than smaller, upstart firms. Basic categories of mutual funds tend to be growth, growth and income, international, and balanced funds. A fund has many benefits over individual stocks, which we'll discuss later in Chapter 9. Spend a little time doing research, sorting available funds based on risk, historical returns, and ratings. Choose one fund you feel comfortable with based on your preferences and money personality. You can also turn to financial news sites such as Kiplinger Magazine and MarketWatch, which analyze and rank funds based on types of features. You can drill down into details for each fund and see many characteristics, such as what they invest in, how long they have been in existence, and who manages the portfolio. Table 6.3 shows the five largest mutual funds based on assets.

Select the firm and the investment that you want to pursue and make an initial investment. Aim for at least $500 to $1,000 if you can afford it—the more, the better. Start investing today. Establish a routine of transferring money directly from your checking account into this investment monthly.

Decision Strategies

How do we do the raise our level of awareness so that we can see the traps and also avoid them? It is extremely difficult to change the lens through which we view our money. Money is sacred to many people, and we are inherently averse to change. As humans, we prefer the default—doing the same thing and not changing what we are currently doing. The *default effect* is when our brain is given a choice between the default (or the usual or standard) and something else, we naturally will gravitate towards the default. This is problematic for raising awareness and is the reason why if we like chocolate ice cream, we may never try new flavors such as buttered pecan or espresso. It is also why we are hesitant to try yogurt instead of ice cream. Anything which holds us to the default our brains are hardwired to prefer. That's why it is so hard to make change in our money management, yet it can be done.

There are a couple of strategies you should try to raise awareness: set an intention, create standard approach and systems, focus on attitudes and habits, and get started today.

Set an Intention

An *intention* is a commitment or a desired state in the future. It helps you to focus on both where you are and where you want to be. An intention could be as simple as "every morning I wake up and look at my finances" or "I will have $5,000 (or whatever goal you set) in an investment account by the end of the year." Intentions should be realistic but also stretch you a little. Intentions are reminders of how you will enable your goals each day. An *affirmation*, or a mantra, is something that you repeat to yourself daily, out loud and within your own head, to provide yourself emotional support and motivation. If we concentrate on these affirmations daily, we can gain insight into our own minds. These affirmations help to reset the behavioral biases and negative thinking from your brain. A mantra could be something like "I am organized and make excellent decisions with my finances" or "I set goals confidently and achieve them with success." Simple words of encouragement will remind you of your journey ahead. To create your own affirmations, stay positive, realistic, and focused on your goals. Your affirmation should make you feel capable and ready for any challenge.

Create a Standard Approach and Systems

Each time you confront a money situation (e.g., at time of a purchase, paying a bill, or considering a new venture), use a common approach. Ask yourself a set of questions and use a checklist to encourage mindfulness. Prepare yourself mentally. Make time to think through your approach at the time of a money decision. Develop a system for managing your financial process.

Focus on Attitude and Habits

You must be in the right mindset to make financial changes. Our self-perception is primarily based on how we feel (emotions) and what we do (behaviors).

Thinking the right thoughts and doing the right things are self-reinforcing. Your attitude has been shown to influence your actions.[56] If you adopt an attitude of openness to financial transformation, discipline, and daily intentions, you will inspire change. Habits are automatic behaviors that we often do without thinking. Focus on identifying your habits and change your attitude.

Get Started Today

Make your initial investment into a mutual fund or other investment today. Don't try to find a reason to delay. What is important is that you get into the habit of investing. Also, financial literacy is important as you progress through the steps of wealth. Read or listen nightly to something that will provide useful information about finances, such as videos, books, and magazines. But you must be aware of the type of content. Look for credible sources, such as Kiplinger Finance, Bloomberg Markets, Wall Street Journal, and others that simply report the financial news instead of exploiting it. The important thing is to look for factual information, such as where you can find better interest rates on your savings account or what happened in the stock market. Appendix B shows a summary of some great resources. Be wary of books and articles claiming to offer a get-rich-quick schemes. You might consider your friends and social relationships to ensure they support you along your journey. Surround yourself with positivity; it is also good to have friends who uphold similar financial values and practice good financial habits. In my research, I have found that you may need to change your environment if you are to make lasting change.

It would be normal for you to be uncertain and anxious at this stage. You may even be unsure of how you can go about financial change. Or maybe you see some opportunities but still don't have excitement or motivation to change. This may be the time to consider a financial coach or advocate you can rely on to help you independently review your strategy and plans.

Table 6.4 summarizes each of the major points outlined in this chapter. We will build on these points for each stage in subsequent chapters.

Take Away

- Once we have become frustrated and motivated to change our financial future, we must become aware of our money mindset.
- Focus on the decision approach and your financial systems.

Table 6.4   Typical Characteristics Found in Step 2 of the Mindful Money Model

Summary	*Get Mindful*
Overall financial profile	Pivoting; becoming conscious and aware of money type and financial condition
Money mindset	Uncertainty
Decision style	Self-reliance
Key strategies	Perform money typology assessment; daily intentions; decision checklists
Financial system	Create a decision approach and organization system
Current behavioral bias	Anchoring, automation, availability default

- Strategies to build mindfulness and awareness (such as daily intentions, mantras, daily reflection, and time) are important to really get us moving forward.
- Avoid anchoring, automation, and availability biases that are common here.

Key Terms

affirmation, anchoring bias, automation bias, availability bias, consciousness, decision approach, default effect, intention, vulnerable

Chapter 7

Step 3 — Get Rid (of Negative Money Habits)

"It is easier to prevent bad habits than to break them."

Benjamin Franklin

In step 3, we focus on getting rid of our negative habits and adopting better ones. Poor (or negative) habits are those that decrease your probability of achieving wealth over time. Poor habits encourage lower levels of discipline and mindfulness, as well as excess. Financial discipline and consistency will help you in this step. This chapter focuses on eliminating habits that keep you stuck and integrating behaviors that move you towards your goals.

Habits

Financial discipline is mindful adherence to your intended allocation plans for spending, savings, investing, and giving of your financial resources. Discipline requires removing bad (or negative, poor) habits from your daily routines. By *habit*, I mean a routine or tendency which we perform on a repeated basis without thinking about it. Habits help speed up our brains' processing power by automating tasks that we otherwise would stop and think about.[57] Habits, just like fear, are useful adaptive mechanisms of the brain. They help us adapt to changes and quickly respond. Some habits are neutral, such as waking up every

DOI: 10.4324/9781003231844-9

morning and having a cup of coffee or being frugal with your money and not spending it.

Then there are the negative habits that keep you stuck in old patterns and work to destroy your financial health. Many people through the years have recognized the importance of unconscious routines which dictate our daily rituals and trying to overcome them. Some habits can destroy us, both financially and medically (e.g., illicit drug use). Financially, we can spend more than we have by overusing credit cards and borrowing more than we need through loans. Think about that. I am still amazed when I think that we are allowed to buy more things than we have in cash. Many people can sell everything they have (car, home, clothing, electronics) and still not have enough money to pay what they owe to creditors. I have taught and coached numerous people with poor financial habits, and their challenges centered around two major categories: (1) *excess*—spending or doing too much relative to their resources—and (2) *time*—preferring to do something now versus in the future.

Carefully review the list of habits in Table 7.1. Place a check by each one of these that apply to you.

Table 7.1   List of Negative Financial Habits

(Instructions: Place a check by each one of these that apply to you.)
☐ Impulse spending, such as at the checkout counter of the grocery store
☐ Buying more when you're down or feel sad to improve your mood
☐ Continuous use of your credit cards with inability to pay them off
☐ Making monthly payments without considering the total financial impact of a large purchase (such as a car payment, student loans)
☐ Not having a budget or not sticking to a budget
☐ Thinking "discipline is for old people," since you will likely get rich quick
☐ Cashing your check immediately and spending it
☐ Routinely spending more than you make
☐ Trying to impress your friends with a new purchase
☐ Blaming your company, spouse, or job for your mistakes
☐ Using your paycheck as the excuse for your current financial condition

☐ Not reconciling or balancing your accounts
☐ Paying for multiple services (e.g., streaming, magazines, television) or other items (such as subscriptions, phone apps) that you don't use
☐ Having negative thoughts when you think of money
☐ Purchasing big-ticket items (such as a car or house) impulsively, without planning or careful consideration
☐ Failing to comparison shop to lower the cost of your highest monthly bills (e.g., cell phone, car insurance) in more than 12 months
☐ Lacking a good system for organizing your finances
☐ Regretting a purchase or choice that you have made, more than once this year
☐ Having no idea what your current balances are in savings or on credit cards
☐ Ignoring bills and statements
☐ Paying yourself last (e.g., spending all your paycheck first and not budgeting savings)
☐ Not having any current specific and quantifiable financial goals
☐ Consistently paying bills late
☐ Not checking your credit report
☐ Paying fees or charges of any kind (including bank fees, check cashing fees, insufficient funds/NSF fees, and interest charges)
☐ Investing in something without fully understanding it (e.g., a business, a lease, stock)
☐ Relying on your parents, family, or friends to bail you out of emergencies routinely
☐ Having little or no interest in your finances
☐ Using a check cashing service
☐ Buying everything new (such as a new cell phone or car) rather than used
☐ Using payday loans or cash advances
☐ Thinking only about the current moment and not the future
☐ Defaulting on a credit card or loan in the past

High-Risk Financial Habits

Do any of these habits resonate with you? If you can identify with more than a couple of these, you must become very serious, very fast about changing your financial habits. You may find nothing wrong with some of these habits, while the impact of other habits and their impacts may be very obvious. Have you heard the saying "bury your head in the sand like an ostrich"? In behavioral finance, we call this the *ostrich effect*—seeing what is in front of you while ignoring what would otherwise be an obviously negative or poor choice or circumstance. Let's avoid the ostrich effect.

All these habits are somewhat destructive or high risk—some more than others. There are 10 significant habits that I want to mention specifically. If any of these apply to you, you must stop them today!

High-Risk Habit #1. Cashing Your Checks

Physically cashing a paycheck each month is a huge behavioral trap. Cash is tactile, and when we can physically have that much money at one time (whether it's $200 or $2,000), it creates a visual image of abundance—even when we might not be in a place of abundance. When we know something is there and available, it is much easier to spend it. When it is safely placed away, we are much less likely to spend it. Instead, always use electronic deposit into an account and resist the urge to take out cash.

High-Risk Habit #2. Failing to Use a Bank Account

Not having a bank or credit union account is a significant negative financial habit. I've worked with several people who avoid banks altogether for various reasons, whether it is due to concerns over the government, risks, safety, or something else. You need a bank account into which you can make free electronic deposits. This must be a top priority to find a trusted bank. Remember to check fee structures for all accounts. If they charge you for deposits, for transfers, for withdrawals—look around for better options. According to the Federal Reserve, there are well over 4,300 commercial banks in the United States alone. Shop around. Look online at www.bankrate.com/banking. Compare the best rates but don't be blinded only by rates. Look for fee structures. Banks charge for all kinds of services that we think are standard (e.g., coming in to a teller versus using an automated teller machine [ATM]; using an ATM more than twice per month; getting basic checkbooks; fees for banks that don't have an electronic deposit). Search around and look for the best trade-off between interest rates paid and fees. More than likely, the fees are much more important than the interest. For example, if you had $10,000 in an account that paid 0.20% versus 0.10%, that amounts to basically $1.7 per month in interest versus $1. Doubling the current interest rate gained you less than $1, whereas fees can easily add up to $10 to $50 per month. In short, focus on fees and interest rates. Try to avoid paying fees of any sort. Credit unions are good options if you qualify. Look around and transfer banks if you find a better option.

High-Risk Habit #3. Using Payday Loans

Another negative habit is to rely on cash loans. These are called "payday" lending or "title loan" stores, which allow you to borrow money temporarily at excessively high rates. If you have received a payday or title loan, you should have received a *consumer disclosure*, which would provide the rates and fees of the services. This is also called "the fine print" and is often glossed over. When they market these services on TV or radio, we hear only about an interest rate (let's say 10%). You think, "Well, if I borrow $300 to pay my credit card, I'll only pay 10%, right?" Wrong. Check all the fees. These companies typically charge for all these items:

- Credit access business fees, which can be 1% of the amount borrowed each day!
- Interest rate fees (8%–20%)
- Lien fees
- Delinquent payment fees
- Dishonored instrument charges

All total, depending on how long you take to re-pay that loan, you can pay well more than **300%** annualized percentage rate on a small loan like $300! They also transact in cash, which makes it easier to spend your money and not have detailed records. Always, always avoid these establishments.

High-Risk Habit #4. Neglecting Insurance

One other major area to focus on is insurance. Until you are very, very wealthy, all of us need insurance—car, house, renters, medical, and life insurance. We will talk more about insurance later, but here, focus on maintaining automobile insurance. Even if you are in a state where it is not required by law, you need it. Accidents which result in bodily injury or property damage (to your car or theirs) can destroy families' financial health. Purchase insurance by shopping around. It is quite common for people I have worked with to pay as much for automobile insurance as they do for the monthly car note. You need to be covered—liability insurance, medical payments, and comprehensive coverage to your own car's damage if you need it—but you have options. There are so many alternatives in insurance that you should receive multiple quotes before deciding which firm to go with. In my own comparisons, I've received quotes for individual coverage to vary from $60 per month to $250 per month, with all the same coverage amounts. There seems to be a lot of room for pricing variability based on the company you select. Again, shop around and compare to get the best rates.

High-Risk Habit #5. Confusing Affordability with Monthly Notes

Another negative habit is to assume you can afford something based on the size of the monthly "payments" (or notes) rather than the total effect on your net worth. One of the biggest shifts we will need to make is to think about money in terms of both net worth and monthly budget (not one or the other). Think about how financial choices relate to your whole picture and not solely payments. Here is an example. If you bought a car on credit, you would have both an auto loan and a monthly payment. Many of us only factor in one side of the equation—the monthly loan payment. We think that is reflective of the new car purchase. We worry about if we can afford this out of our current salary. But that's only one side of the equation. The real impact of the purchase has multiple layers such as (1) How does it affect your monthly expenditures? (2) How does it affect your real net worth or equity? and (3) What are you giving up by spending that monthly payment on a car versus something else? You have a big debt that is due, backed up only by the value of the car, and in addition, you still must make monthly payments. You might need to forego a vacation, a home repair, or a medical procedure.

When you think of this in terms of interconnectedness, you put things into perspective, and you weigh the trade-offs. Okay, so you get a new car, but you also get a new giant loan. You also get large monthly payments. You lose out on the opportunity to use that monthly payment for investing, giving, or savings. Consider my mindful money allocation towards spending (and debt). Should you really take this on? Interconnectedness makes you think through the bigger impact. Your overall philosophy shifts should be towards seeing more opportunities, and less constraints.

High-Risk Habit #6. Not Monitoring Your Credit Reports

Per federal law, you are entitled to a free annual copy of your credit report with each or the three major credit agencies (these are listed in Appendix B). Or you can go to annualcreditreport.com and do it in one place. Make sure that you recognize all of the "open" accounts. Double check that credit cards or loans you might have closed and paid off have zero balances and show that you are not in default or arrears. You should be monitoring your credit reports as frequently as possible and even signing up for credit alerts. Make sure that nobody else has assumed your identity and used your information for credit. Utilize the freezing mechanism if needed to temporarily suspend new activity on your accounts. Your credit report is essential to new loans and credit, so make sure that it is correct and dispute those which are in error.

High-Risk Habit #7. Forgetting to Cancel Services

We often stop using items and services we have purchased but neglect to call, email, or click to cancel those services. Charges will continue to stack up until action is taken. If you don't need something, cancel it and make sure the recurring payments stop immediately. Wealthy people do not make payments for things they don't use.

High-Risk Habit #8. Skipping Required Payments

I get it. Sometimes we just don't have enough money to cover all our bills. Choices are made about priorities. What you should never do is to completely skip payments. Many people just stop paying their bills for housing rent or mortgage, their car loans, or any other bill. Wealthy people pay their bills on time, and they do not skip payments. A much more successful habit involves contacting the creditor (or landlord) and making arrangements in advance for partial payments or an agreement to defer. Don't just let payments go by and continue to shred the invoices and statements. This is a high-risk habit which will land you in financial jeopardy. Make plans and arrangements. You will be surprised how often people are willing to work with you to re-structure your agreements.

High-Risk Habit #9. Thinking Bankruptcy Is a Viable Option

There are multiple types of bankruptcies, some which try to sell your assets and pay back your debts; others eliminate certain kind of debts. Attorneys who work in this area will encourage people who are financially behind to declare bankruptcy. Of course, their legal fees will be paid. Who loses out? You do. Not only is your credit worthiness completely damaged for many years, but you also have shown that you don't have the mental persistence and discipline to work through your challenges. Does a marathon runner quit the race when they see somebody take the lead? Wealthy people generally do not file bankruptcy. Bankruptcy should always be your last resort.

High-Risk Habit #10. No Plans for Medical Expenses

Medical expenses are the number one reason people go bankrupt in the United States. Health insurance is expensive. The Affordable Care Act has helped to make it more widely available on the marketplace, but it can still be costly. Have a plan for medical coverage. If you have the option for employer-sponsored coverage, take it. Check out Medicaid or Medicare coverage if available to you. If not, look at the healthcare.gov website and find a plan in your area. One client of mine did not have insurance and lost his right hand while mowing a yard as a contractor. The emergency department and surgery invoices were $25,000—which are actually pretty low considering some prices for hospitals. What if COVID-19 forced you into an intensive care unit for 30 days, at a cost of over $1 million? Prioritize this expense and proactively have a strategy for your medical expenses and coverage.

Mindful Practice 21   Document, rank, and attack your negative habits.

CASE IN POINT

Margaret T. worked as an acupuncturist and holistic medicine provider. She was very caring and compassionate, which was ideal for her field, but admittedly, she was not good with managing her money. She sub-leased a small 400-square-foot office in an inexpensive part of town. Generally, she spent less than she brought in and was paying herself a small salary. One day she woke up and decided to move locations. She found and leased a new larger property (2,000 square feet) in a different part of the city. When I examined it, the net lease was nearly triple what she was currently paying per month and well more than she could afford. She hadn't yet started to see any increase in clients, mainly because she hadn't started her marketing efforts. Most important, without any planning, she hadn't saved any cash for emergency reserves for this move. Within three months, she had to back out of the lease, which cost her significantly in terms of both lost cash and marketing dollars. To fund it, she took out a line of credit at an extremely high interest rate to get out of the mistake. Lack of financial discipline and careful preparation before big money choices are two of the most common negative habits we must break.

Attacking Negative Habits

Now regardless of how many items you identified with earlier in Table 7.1, the process is the same: identify (document), prioritize (rank), and overcome (attack) your self-perceived negative habits. Place a check mark on every one of the rows which you identify with; then go line by line and prioritize those that you checked.

The highest priority (1) would indicate something which you do nearly all of the time and has a negative impact on your financial wealth. Rank the top 10 of all the habits you selected. Rank as most important those which you believe you could do first and have the greatest impact.

After you rank and prioritize, you must start attacking the habits. How? Well, it all depends on which ones. Some of them are quite easy to do. I would start with ones that are manageable, and importantly, do not tackle all of them at once. Focus on a few or a handful so that you don't get discouraged. Work on one, then another, and after a few weeks or months, work up to handling more. This is where your new mindset will come in useful. Don't get discouraged and don't stop if you have an unsuccessful day or week. If you tried to curb your impulse buys yet you found yourself with a new dress when you went to go buy a t-shirt, don't get discouraged. See if the item can be returned. If not, focus on today and the future and not the past. Learn the lesson and move forward.

Also as discussed earlier, building wealth is about clarity and reducing fear. Clarity—or being clear, lucid, and transparent—has also been shown to be

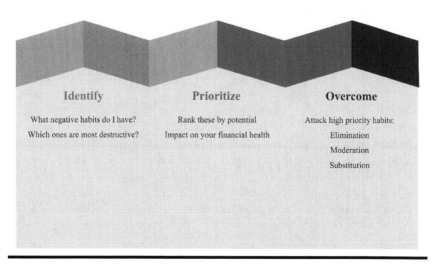

Figure 7.1 How to Confront Negative Financial Habits.

associated with shorter times to adopt better habits.[58] The clearer you can be about your intended habit, the better off you will be. If you use vague phrases, such as "I will try to reduce my impulse purchases at the grocery store," you will likely not see any change. If you can clarify that with "I will completely stop . . . " or "I will reduce by $50 my amount of purchases . . . " you will achieve much better results.

There are three general strategies for getting rid of negative habits:

1. Elimination
2. Moderation
3. Substitution

Elimination

The first and arguably most difficult strategy is to completely eliminate the negative financial habit. *Elimination* is the complete removal or avoidance of the negative habit in its entirety. If you think about this in terms of health or social habits, such as quitting smoking, this could be a difficult task, especially if the habit is one which is so engrained in your way of being that you associate yourself with the habit. If you think that "coffee is life" and every day post to your social media a picture of you visiting a coffee shop and sharing a cup of coffee with the barista, well, this habit is engrained a little more permanently. That would take more time, since coffee is now equated to your perceptions of what you should be doing and has been elevated to being something extremely important.

But if you could simply stop doing something, it would probably have the biggest impact on your wallet. For example, if you eat out every meal and spend $10 per meal, you might simply stop altogether and see what alternatives exist (e.g., packing your own lunch). If this were something you could do, this would likely have the best results.

Now instead of coffee or lunch, think about whatever habit you have selected and see if there are alternatives to eliminate it completely. That could be "making impulse purchases," or you're a person that prides themselves on never thinking about money. Whatever it is, elimination can be difficult. If you can separate the habit from who you are and what you do daily, you will be much more likely to be able to stop doing it.

If you are going to eliminate something, it might also be useful to write down the habit to bring more clarity to it. For instance, putting a note inside your wallet near the credit card that says "No Impulse Purchases" will remind you at checkout to put back certain items you probably don't need. Or simply "Cancel cable subscription by 3 p.m. today" will prompt you to do so. Making sure that you purchase from a written down list, such as when you go to a grocery store, also makes sure that you cut back on last-minute purchases.

You might consider even adding key reminders and alerts to your calendar daily. Write it down to bring specificity to it and make it more permanent.

Moderation

Other times we may choose to cut back but don't necessarily eliminate something. *Moderation* is the partial minimization and removal of some of the excess and extreme impact of the negative financial habit. I work with people who have difficulty with substance use disorders, and many times they work on habits that involve moderation rather than completely cutting out certain substances. Others choose full-out elimination and believe moderation is simply tolerating the same behavior—which, it is, but from a financial perspective, our goal is not necessarily to eliminate everything but to eliminate that which hurts your chances of finding wealth. You will decide what works best for you. If you can completely eliminate it, this strategy is probably the best. But if moderation (or limiting and cutting back the quantity) can help move you in the right direction, then do that.

You may need a combination of both to move towards your goals.

Substitution

As you work through these habits, it may not be in your best interest to try to either completely repress or hold back your strong feelings about a loss of something or even moderate that loss. You might have tried cutting back on things or eliminating, but neither worked because you had a strong emotional attachment to the item. *Substitution* is the act of replacing one habit for another one that moves you towards your goals. For example, let's say that you really enjoy the diversity and flexibility of offerings by having access

> *Document all streaming, subscription, and mobile app services. You will be surprised how many you might have.*

to six different streaming services (e.g., Disney, Netflix, HBO Max, Apple TV), yet the monthly cost is now adding up to over $100. You would like to cut back on half of that but can't seem to do it. Having negative thoughts about "losing" these services and ruminating over these feelings will only result in negative sentiment that will stay with you for a long time (i.e., loss aversion bias). We all have a general tendency to want to keep things the same and not lose something that we once treasured. A better option might to be find a new service at the same time that might be free or much less expensive. So, while you gave up the Amazon Prime and HBO Max, you replaced them with a less expensive streaming service. Finding a way to substitute a less expensive but similar quality service or item can help ease the behavioral impact on all of us. Try substituting or swapping out some negative habits with alternatives rather than cutting out entirely or just cutting back.

Get Independent Help

At this stage, you have been identifying, prioritizing, and working to eliminate, moderate, or substitute negative habits while learning new and better habits which will eventually replace the negative ones. At this point, you might feel overwhelmed. It is a lot to try to do all of this on your own. This is a good time to consider use of a financial coach, advisor, or advocate who you can talk to. This could be somebody at your work or church, but they need to be independent to help you bring clarity to your spending and to your goals. A financial advisor or coach who you hire should be what is called *fee only*; this ensures that the method of compensating the advisor is aligned with yours as a *fiduciary* (meaning they have your best financial interest in mind). Some advisors, such as advisors at an insurance company, might be more economically incentivized to sell you a product than to tell you to eliminate or cut back on something. In this case, they may not give you the best advice or tips. You need to make sure whoever you select is representing your best interest and not simply taking a commission for their sales.

To help you find an advisor, look at the various links in Appendix B for finding a planner, coach, or advisor. The terms are fairly interchangeable although there are licensing guidelines for those people called investment advisors. Any outside independent help will be good, but especially if you find somebody with training in behavioral finance who can address behavioral issues that might be limiting your financial potential. Ask them the following questions, including are you a fiduciary? Are you fee only, or are you receiving any commissions for your recommendations? Are you limited on the mutual funds or investments you can offer? What designations and degrees do you have that qualify you as an advisor? How do you normally work with your clients?

If you can find one who is acceptable and you like their answers, go ahead and hire them. Working with an advisor can help in multiple ways. They can help you find and purchase insurance. They can review your budget and spending. And they can help create a financial plan for the four key financial decision categories (spending, saving, investing, and giving), which will be important in the next stage.

Behavioral Traps

Hopefully, as we rid ourselves of negative habits, we can see more opportunities and alternatives. Of course, you still have a lot of work ahead of you. You are beginning the process of financial change!

You will likely confront multiple behavioral traps in this step. One is your natural preference towards not losing any of your built-up assets and burying your head in the sand regarding certain behaviors. *Loss aversion* for savings and investments suggests that you'd rather not gain as much on the upside to minimize any losses. But we tend to also bury our heads in the sand and would rather ignore problem areas than fix them (the *ostrich effect*). We must worry about both of those as we begin shedding poor financial behaviors. It remains important not to let either of these two biases sink in.

Past financial mistakes (whether chronic or one time) should help you gain additional perspective and knowledge. Try to learn something from each of them. Some of the people I've observed have blown so much money, and they can't overcome that feeling of regret. If this sounds familiar, you must be able to get beyond it. Learn from your mistakes but don't dwell on them excessively—document what you should take away and strip out the important lesson. If you bought a new vehicle you can't afford, separate the "emotion" from the "lesson." The learning is before you purchase something big, you have some homework to do first. Carefully review loan options, interest rates, payments, your current balance, your monthly obligations, and the impact this will have on your net worth. The emotion is that feeling every time you see the car. The car is not the issue; the lack of planning and impulsive purchasing is. In behavioral finance, we have a term called *sunk cost*, which is an expense that has already been incurred and cannot be reversed. It does no good to continue to contemplate "what if I wouldn't have made that purchase?," or "what could I have done with that money?" The fact is, that decision is behind you. You need to look forward. Learn from the mistake, don't repeat it, and look forward.

Mindful Practice 22   Expose, don't bury, past financial mistakes.

HEALTHY HABIT STRATEGIES

As you build clarity and focus, you have identified some habits which might be holding you back. You are now aware of them and have prioritized them. This is the start of your financial plan, which will need to be documented and executed. You will notice that even the relatively small choices need to be elevated to the conscious level at this point if you are going to take any action.

To get out of this stage, though, you can follow some of these strategies.

1. **Utilize a personal finance devotional.** Daily, wake up and spend a few minutes clarifying your intention for the day related to personal finance. Such as "Today I will get my bills in order" or "Today I will call my bank about savings options." Maintaining a list of these priority items in a journal would be a great idea to get clear and specific.
2. **Get something; sell something.** For every "new" thing you purchase, try to sell or cancel something else. For every new suit or jacket I purchase, I usually donate or sell one. Don't just keep adding to your expenses and purchases without trying. Wealth is not about accumulation of things but rather a mindful mix of choices.
3. **Take off your blinders.** Remind yourself to look thoroughly at your patterns of spending, saving, and investing. Take off your blinders to avoid the common biases in this stage and look for all options and alternatives that are available to you.
4. **Adopt healthier money habits.** Be sure to avoid the 10 high-risk negative habits. Find some healthy financial habits that you can devote time to each day. Allow time for the healthy habits to replace the negative ones.

Table 7.2 summarizes each of the major points outlined in this chapter. We will build on this for each stage in subsequent chapters.

Table 7.2   Typical Characteristics Found in Step 3 of the Mindful Money Model

Summary	Get Rid (of Negative Habits)
Overall financial profile	Shedding; learning financial discipline; using budgeting tools
Money mindset	Gaining financial discipline
Decision style	Introspective
Key strategies	Prioritization of negative habits
Financial system	Use personal finance devotional; daily journal
Current behavioral bias	Loss, aversion, ostrich effect, sunk cost fallacy

Take Away

- To achieve wealth, we must rid ourselves of negative financial habits that might destroy our quest.
- There are at least 10 extremely high-risk habits we must avoid altogether.
- Use one of three strategies for negative habits: elimination, moderation, or substitution.
- Bring clarity to habits by writing them down, being specific, and putting them on calendars and reminders.
- The use of a daily financial decision journal will help crystallize the changes internally and prepare you for what is next.

Key Terms

bankruptcy, consumer disclosure, elimination, fee only, financial discipline, habit, loss aversion bias, moderation, ostrich effect, substitution, sunk cost

Chapter 8

Step 4 — Get Specific

"I don't focus on what I'm up against. I focus on my goals, and I try to ignore the rest."

Venus Williams

Are you ready to get down to numbers? The next step in our quest is to get specific about dollars and cents. Armed with a better awareness of our money mindset and after mitigating some of our negative habits, we focus now on becoming very specific about our goals, intentions, and current finances. This is a bit more detailed step because we have overcome the "low-hanging fruit" and need to address our deeper financial patterns. Getting focused requires us to get a clear picture of our spending priorities and our short-term financial goals and to develop a vision of where we want to be. This chapter aims to de-mystify the financial planning process and focus our efforts on the most important aspects of the plan. There are also multiple templates, resources, and tools to get us started.

Financial Goals and Guesses

There are so many good reasons to create a financial plan: to build a retirement nest egg, to buy a new home, to plan for you or your children's future educational needs, or even to support your parents when they get older. All of these are useful for specific purposes. Yet financial planning is not just about preparing for major life events or purchases. I view *financial planning* as a systematic roadmap for financial decision-making. This roadmap helps to guide us, keep us on track, and ensure that our choices are aligned with a strategic perspective of where we are heading. This is useful because as we have seen, behaviors and emotions impact our judgment and choice, which often results in a pattern of choices that are not in sync with what we once intended.

Financial planning can help to create a better understanding of your short- and long-term goals. The Certified Financial Planner Board of Standards defines it as "looking at a client's entire financial picture and advising them on how to achieve their short- and long-term financial goals."[59]

The core focus of financial planning is to express and then realize your goals. *Goals* are desired results or specific intentions you hope to achieve. Goals should be concrete and as specific as possible. In order to have a goal, you must have an *intention*—something in the future you intend to accomplish or achieve. We talked about intentions earlier and the power that they play in changing our mindset.

Financial goals are worthwhile, and I support the notion of expressing your goals as clearly as you can. But on the other hand, do you really know how to answer some of the questions that are required to establish a goal?

For example, let's say you want to be able to stop working at age 50 to move to Europe and travel and be free. Sounds like a good plan to me! Now, a financial advisor would ask you to put that into numbers. How much would that cost? Well, we can guess all day long how much an extended stay hotel might cost us (converting that into Euros) and estimate a typical cost for food and laundry and other essentials. Or we could use a heuristic to estimate needs, such as 80% of your current salary per year. We could even try to adjust for currency fluctuations. We would indeed end up with a number and then multiply that out for the number of years you intend to travel and come up with a reasonably sound goal.

How realistic is that really? Do we know how much we might want to spend when we're not working? We live life in the present and understand historical costs only in the future. We are horrible at predicting things, and really the actual figures are so far away from our guesses that if we measured them, we would likely see 100%+ errors on all of them.

There is another reason to be worried about goals in general. Goals are like milestones; they change once we reach them. Think about it. Your goal when we were in high school was to graduate and maybe get a job or go to college. So, you got through that goal, what then? Well hopefully, you set another goal, such as making a certain amount of money. Or finding an ideal spouse. Or buying a home in a great neighborhood. What if you are in retirement? What's your goal?

The point is not that making specific goals is not important. They are. We must remember though that goals change constantly, and numbers need to continuously be updated to reflect them. And as we have seen, our brains often try to reduce their load by shortcutting certain tasks. So, in the process of trying to create financial goals, we really are producing at best, a guess. A financial goal is our best guess as to what our ambitions might require.

Therefore, the system (i.e., the process involved in thinking through our choices and estimating our future ambitions) and approach are much more important than the specific number. When you see those commercials on television that say "What is your number?" and it's asking how much you need for retirement, just keep in mind that while it is nice to know, it really is just your best guess at that moment in time.

Barriers to Planners and Planning

Many people avoid financial advisors because they believe the process involved for financial planning is overwhelming or anxiety producing. It also requires you to share a lot of confidential information, which makes some people nervous. People also tend to feel judged. You might feel that you already have it under control. There have been a number of studies looking at why people don't engage more with financial professionals, and the bottom line is this: most people don't use a planner, and most people do not have a financial plan. Recent surveys I have seen suggest that most (upwards of nearly ¾ of the population) do not use outside financial assistance.[60] Of those who do use a planner, nearly half think they are too expensive.[61] Yet despite all these barriers, do you know who does have a planner and a plan? The wealthy. And those that are about to become wealthy.

Financial planning doesn't have to be stressful. I strongly suggest, despite your rationale for avoiding them, finding an independent financial coach or planner to help guide you through the process. An advisor can be the independent voice that listens and offers recommendations to help you achieve the goals you are expressing. An advisor also help to implement the plans by setting up policies and accounts. This is often needed at this step in the journey because it is easier to dream about the future than do the tasks necessary today to make that happen.

That being said, you can create and execute your own financial plan if you follow the steps outlined in this chapter.

The Financial Planning Process

The process of financial planning is really about setting goals, acting on these goals, and shoring up any areas of weakness. Figure 8.1 shows the core components of the process.

1. Visioning (creating a shared vision of the future with specific, quantifiable goals)
2. Mobilizing (gathering and quantifying your historical data and numbers)
3. Sequencing (identifying and targeting gaps)
4. Monitoring (sticking to the plan)

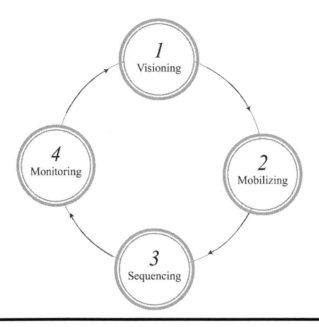

Figure 8.1 Financial Planning Process.

I will describe the first two steps in this chapter (visioning and mobilizing). The next two (sequencing and monitoring) are covered in Chapter 9.

Visioning

Dream big. We need to begin a process of planning. Since financial planning revolves around a roadmap for goals, it requires you to focus on the future. Yet as we discussed, many people avoid thoughts of their future for behavioral, emotional, or just pure practical matters. *Visioning*, or envisioning, is a process of imagination and goal-setting. In order to do this properly, you must imagine the following types of questions and scenarios:

- Where will I be in the next two years? How about 20 years?
- Will I be married?
- Will I have children? How many? How old?
- Will my parents be able to support themselves as they get older?
- What are the major events which I need to consider?

Many of these answers require you to consider your ultimate purpose—your "why" as many call it. *Why* is defined as a "compelling higher purpose that inspires us and acts as the source of all we do."[62] Part of this imagination or inspiration has to center around your emotional and spiritual well-being, health, and relationships. Where do you want to live? Who do you want to be? What do you want to achieve? Dream big!

Mindful Practice 23 Write down specific goals and hold yourself accountable.

Part of it, though, needs to be grounded in your profession and work, which ultimately leads to your finances. If you can't pay for your dreams, they will never become a reality. The process of envisioning what your life will look like might result in a different career path, promotions, changes in salary, or relocation to different geographical places of employment. When you set out to create this vision, I recommend writing it down, such as in a vision diagram or a template (Table 8.1).

Table 8.1 Financial Planning—Vision Template

Name:	_____	Date: _____
1.	What am I really good at?	
2.	What do I care about the most?	
3.	What do I want to be doing differently?	
4.	What could be the expected timeline for this?	
5.	What impact might it have on my financial picture?	
6.	What challenges stand in my way?	
7.	What are the key milestones between now and then?	
8.	What are steps I can take today to move me in that direction?	

Once you have contemplated your vision, it is important to note that this is not set in stone. It might not be permanent for your entire life and will likely change as you age. But keep track of it. Document it in your financial journal.

Mindful Practice 24   Dream big. Then take small steps each day!

Now our goal is to articulate that vision into financial terms by translating it into short- and long-term financial needs and goals.

CASE IN POINT

John B. is a 36-year-old technology consultant who had been serving as a project manager for software implementations for the past decade. After his two daughters got close to graduating high school, he recognized that he never thought about his family's financial priorities and goals. He has a total of $25,000 in a money market mutual fund and $6,000 in a joint checking account. He is now questioning how he can afford college tuition for his children.

Setting Financial Goals

Research on goal setting shows that the more specific you can be in articulating your intentions, the more likely you are to hit these goals and then the more you are likely to stretch these goals to continue to outperform.[63] Others have shown that motivation and goals are tightly linked, so the higher the levels of motivation, the more likely you are to achieve precisely defined goals.[64]

It is important that as living, breathing humans, we continuously grow and challenge ourselves. No matter where we are in life, we should have an additional goal to strive for. That is something which separates us from normal mammals and other animals: we have brains that are always wanting to grow and expand and strive for more. It doesn't have to be a complicated goal. It could be "To maintain the same standard of living I have now through 20 years post-retirement."

It could also be much more demanding, such as "To earn $200,000 per year for the next 10 years." The key to goals are to have some specificity to them (quantifiable as much as possible, with dates) with the understanding that they are just point estimates in time. I prefer to clarify three aspects to a financial goal:

1. What is your goal, specifically?
2. Why do you want to achieve it?
3. By when?

For example, try filling in Table 8.2 with regards to your own personal finance goals. Use the first blank to indicate something specific with regards to the four money choices (buy, give, invest, or spend). The second blank should be your best estimate of a date. The third blank gives you space to articulate why you want to do this. All three are important. For example:

> *"I want to <u>purchase a $25,000 BMW</u> convertible sportscar this time next year on <u>December 3,</u> because <u>this is the car of my dreams,</u> and I want to drive the entire Pacific Coast Highway in it."*

When I started out in business and was investing and saving, my only goal was to "be rich." It had no specific meaning or purpose. I didn't even know what "rich" meant. Maybe being a millionaire would have been more quantifiable, but then I didn't even have any concept of what a million dollars meant. As children, we only know what symbols and images we see on movies and videos. It took me years of research and reading and working with others to be able to short-cut the goal setting to those simple statements.

If you can fill that in with those well-conceived goals, you will be substantially ahead of most people. Well-articulated goals can be both visualized and realized.

Table 8.2   Articulating Your Financial Goals

Goal #1	I want to _____ by _____ because _____ _____.
Goal #2	I want to _____ by _____ because _____ _____.
Goal #3	I want to _____ by _____ because _____ _____.

Mindful Practice 25   Financial goals change, and so must your plan.

Your primary challenge is to specifically identify all financial impacts related to the vision and a list of concrete goals and action items that will move your vision forward. The process for setting goals is really simple: **identify, prioritize, monetize**.

- **Identify your goals.** Make a list of all goals using the prior template, such as a wedding, vacation, college, or education, moving to a new city, adopting a child, or starting a business. Write these down in a journal or an electronic document. The process of writing down goals helps you to clarify your intentions and crystallize them into your identity and beliefs.
- **Prioritize your goals.** Organize them by what is the most important to you. Which goal helps you move the needle a little closer to your vision? Write down specific dates and timelines for each of them.
- **Monetize the goals.** Being as specific as possible, *monetize* (or determine the financial implications) each of these goals. This will help you understand cash flow requirements by dates.

Figure 8.2 outlines the goal setting process.

Financial Goal Setting

- ○ Outline your vision
- ○ Set Goals: identify, prioritize, monetize
- ○ Plan for the financial impact
- ○ Document needs and gaps
- ○ Create specific action items
- ○ Make consistent choices

Figure 8.2   Financial Goal-Setting Checklist.

Short- and Long-term Goals

You will need to translate your specific vision into some both short- and long-term goals. I think the key to achieving anything really big is to set your sights partially on the big picture and partially on the next step. Keep one eye on the horizon (big picture) and one on the ground (near-term). Setting these goals will help you create action items and plans for hitting them. Specifically, look for any impacts that can be quantified. Ask yourself, what are the expected returns or tradeoffs from this vision? What are the cash flow needs and requirements? Try to be as specific as possible using dates and a timeline to keep you on track.

As an example, let's say your vision involves moving to a new city to live. Your homework items include researching the cost-of-living difference between your new city and where you currently live. You would need to look at all expenses required for packing and moving, buying, or renting a new home, as well as other costs you will incur.

Offensive and Defensive Financial Strategies

Depending on where you are at in your quest towards wealth, you may have different types of strategies and goals. At times you want to protect what you have, and other times you may want to go all out and be aggressive. I like to categorize these as defensive and offensive strategies. An offensive financial strategy would be focused on capitalizing on your strengths as well as the market opportunities. A defensive strategy would be more likely to defend against losses and preserve your current financial position. Defensive strategies include insurance and risk management.

There are important linkages between your money type and tolerance for risk (i.e., aggressive, conservative, moderate investing) and your stage in the wealth life cycle (retirement vs. early career building). Re-visit the money typology discussed earlier to recall your preferences towards risk and decisions. The concept of offensive and defensive strategy can apply everywhere, in your savings, spending, and giving as well as investments.

An *offensive* financial strategy focuses on your strengths. If you have a strength in understanding certain markets (like technology or healthcare), then you would concentrate your investments in that area. Target investments more assertively in areas that you know well. Avoid investing in areas you don't know much about—that makes you much more vulnerable and in a weaker position.

Offensive strategies also uses any early advantage. If you see the market is down, you will invest—not hold back. A defensive strategy would do the opposite. It would refrain from investing when the market is down. Offensive would also exploit what others are NOT doing. Warren Buffett, one of the world's leading investors, is said to often go against the trend. A defensive strategy would likely yield to what others are doing.

Offensive strategies tend to be those that are not as easy to imitate. You would be a little more aggressive in savings and investing in higher-risk opportunities and a little less focused relatively on defending your current wealth. An offensive tax strategy would also take measures to reduce future tax liabilities, while a defensive one might focus more on reducing taxes paid today only.

A *defensive* strategy tends to take a "wait and see" approach. It would also focus on protecting current financial position. A little more conservative, a little more focused on preservation. Insurance, to defend against all types of loses, is much more likely in a defensive position. Home, auto, life, and especially personal liability insurance would be maximized to reduce any potential exposures.

A defensive strategy would also likely focus on more consistent, lower-risk savings and investment opportunities. Increasing post-retirement savings would likely be more important than liquid, marketable assets. Plans for distributing wealth and giving are more likely to happen as a defensive strategy as well.

Figure 8.3 presents a snapshot of offensive and defensive financial strategies.

We will come back to the idea of offensive and defensive strategies in subsequent chapters. It is important to note that you don't need to be entirely offensive or defensive with your finances. At certain times in life, we are definitely more defensive. You need a healthy combination of both, but it needs to be aligned with your risk and money personality type. Otherwise, an offensive strategy would cause a risk-averse person to be continuously in a state of angst. And vice versa. A completely defensive strategy would likely make the assertive and aggressive money types feel frustrated or bored. Sometimes we must take a defensive approach, while other times we take more of an offensive strategy.

Mobilizing

In this second major step of the financial planning process, there are two key activities: (1) collecting all of your historical financial data and (2) turnings them into financial statements. To start, pull out all paperwork you might have filed away, as well as your account user information for bank, insurance, and online accounts so that you can pull the most recent statements. *Mobilizing* is the process of gathering and assembling all important financial information about what you spend, what you own, and who and how much you owe. Figure 8.4 shows some of the important information you will need to collect.

These data points will be extremely useful for putting together the most important financial statements and analyzing your financial ratios (we will discuss both of these later). Even if you don't have these statements put together, you

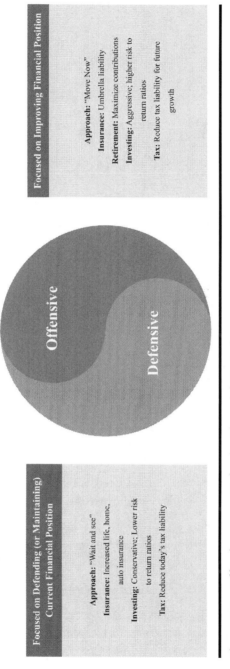

Figure 8.3   Offensive versus Defensive Financial Strategies.

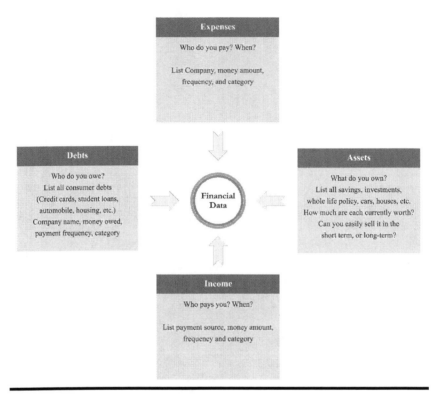

Figure 8.4 Mobilize Your Financial Data.

have the information necessary to create them. They are not difficult to create, but they do take some data gathering. The two statements we will assemble are

1. **A budget.** This is a detailed and itemized listing of all expenses and revenue for a certain time period, usually monthly.
2. **A statement of net worth.** This is a summary of your personal balance sheet, which describes what you own and what you owe at any given point in time, usually the beginning of each month.

Itemized Expense and Revenue Budget

Everybody needs a budget. A *budget* is a written estimate of your planned expenses (cash going out) and revenue (cash coming in) over a specific period of time (usually monthly or quarterly). The only way to create a budget, though, is to completely understand your past patterns of spending and receiving money.

If we tried to put together a budget based on our recollection of what we thought we spent, we would significantly undervalue certain types of expenses and overstate others. This is that recall bias we talked about earlier. We may not even have an idea of the total we are spending each month, let alone at specific category levels. A budget and corresponding itemized inventory of transactions is the foundation of all financial plans.

Let's start though with the money that you have coming in each month. This is usually easier for most people than the expenses. Source of cash inflow tend to be

- Your paycheck
- Bonuses or tips received
- Social security payments
- IRS stimulus check or tax refunds
- Interest income from your bank accounts
- Dividends or capital gains on any investments
- Royalties (if you had mineral rights)
- Sales of any personal assets
- Rental property income
- Any other money received (e.g., gambling, inheritance)

For most of us, our salary is our primary source of cash, and all the other areas are much less. But for others, such as those in retirement, investment dividends and Social Security might be the largest categories. You need to capture all of these to get the best picture of your money coming in.

For some of you, the salary will be easy to estimate, especially if you are only paid once or twice per month. But for others who receive payments for services provided or are an independent contractor, you will need to spend some time looking at your cash coming in. Add these up for a period of at least two months. If one month it is $4,000, the next is $2,500, and the third month is $3,900, use an average of these unless you have some reason to suspect that future months will be lower or higher. Once you get the hang of this, you will want to continue doing it every month though.

Your budgeted expenses are considered cash outflows or outlays. They are the sources of your expenditures and include everything you buy, lease, rent, consume, or are taxed on. For a period of time, you will need to keep a very detailed list of every dollar that you spend over at least 60 days. It needs to be a period long enough to capture all expenses you would normally incur. If you did this for a small business, you'd need to track it even longer because most expenses are seasonal in some businesses and only occur every few months. I prefer using a journal to write down all transactions as they occur, so you don't forget any

What I Spend Each Day					
Date	Time	Money Amount	Category	Purpose	Cash/Credit
March 2	10:15 am	$3.28	Food	Coffee	Cash
March 2	3:47 pm	$12.95	Supplies	Pens	Credit
March 2	7:12 pm	$5.00	Entertainment	Movie	Cash
March 4	8:30 am	$87.23	Groceries	Food	Credit
March 5	6:22 pm	$43.20	Cell phone	Monthly phone	Cash

Figure 8.5 Itemized Expense Tracking.

expense. I've worked with some people who thought they could remember what they did by the end of the day, but you'd be surprised how your brain, working unconsciously for the most part, spends small amounts of money without registering in your longer-term memory. So, track even the smallest expense, such as that spent at the donut shop or the convenience store.

Keep in mind that this budget reflects all of your cash outlays. There are some excellent expense tracking software tools out there, including those on the internet or available for your personal computer or mobile phone. In Appendix B, there is a list of some good applications you can use if you prefer to track on your phone, such as Mint and Quicken. If you prefer to record them manually, you can use a ledger or notebook to record your expenses. Figure 8.5 shows a sample daily recordkeeping journal you can use to record all expenses.

Budgeting 1, 2, 3

Once you have recorded all of your expenses and revenue for a period of time (preferably a month or two), you need to start work on the budget. Here are the specific steps for creating your budget.

1. Daily use the itemized expense tracking form shown for a period of 4–8 weeks to get a reasonable sample of your spending patterns.
2. Sum up all similar expenses into the categories from that form (such as rent, food, and so on).
3. Add the total of all expenses on a per month basis. This is best done if you put it into a spreadsheet. This total represents the amount of money you spend monthly.

4. Add up all of your sources of income monthly. If you work in a position or are self-employed, where you don't have regular, fixed payments, you will need to look back at prior periods to estimate how much income you bring in per month.

5. Subtract out the cash outflows from cash received to get to net disposable income or net cash flow for each period (I will call this "reserve" for simplicity). This difference is the amount of money in reserve which you have for investing, saving, or giving (the other three primary money decisions besides spending).

6. Calculate what percentage of your total income you have in reserve (or net cash flow). We will talk about that more in the following section on money allocation.

7. Look at all spending categories and target opportunities for cost-cutting. Consider the negative habits we explored in Chapter 7.
   a. In which areas are you over-spending?
   b. What areas are you most surprised about?
   c. What can you do to take corrective actions? Can you change your cell phone service? Cancel a digital movie or TV subscription?

8. Once you have tracked all expenditures and have a really good understanding of where you are currently spending, create a target budget by category. This should be a fixed $ amount goal per month that you can save by category and in total. This will become your "target budget."

9. Your target budget needs to take into account all of the removal of the negative habits and adoption of the healthy habits.

10. The difference between your current and actual budget is the incremental (net reserve) amount you can add to savings, retirement, education planning, moving, or any other goals you identified in the visioning and goal-setting process.

To help show you a more complete list of categories that most people typically use, refer to Table 8.3. If there are other areas not listed that you find yourself spending money on, add them into your specific budget.

The target category reflects how you think you can reduce or eliminate some of the expenses in the actual column of this table. If you can cut out $100 from subscriptions, for example, you would have $100 lower in the target budget and the same amount net cash flow.

> *Money in (revenues) – Money out (expenses) = Net cash flow*

After you have worked through the expenses and the budget, we will examine the difference between revenues and expenses. This leaves us with net cash flow, or reserves, which can be used to contribute towards the goals you have outlined in your new vision and to invest, save, and give.

Table 8.3 Monthly Expense Budget

Expense Type	Actual Payment, monthly $	Target Budget, monthly $	Variance	% of Total Monthly Expense
Mortgage (principal and interest) or rent payments	$	$	%	$
Real estate property taxes	$	$	%	$
Home insurance	$	$	%	$
Food (groceries)	$	$	%	$
Entertainment (restaurants, bars, concerts)	$	$	%	$
Electricity, utilities	$	$	%	$
Cable, digital subscriptions (internet, books, videos)	$	$	%	$
Automobile lease or payment	$	$	%	$
Auto gasoline, tolls, parking, public transportation	$	$	%	$
Auto insurance	$	$	%	$
Cell phones, TV subscriptions	$	$	%	$
Childcare, toys, school activities	$	$	%	$
Education, tuition, books	$	$	%	$
Home maintenance, cleaning	$	$	%	$
Memberships	$	$	%	$
Life, property, liability insurance	$	$	%	$
Healthcare, physicians, Rx	$	$	%	$
Shopping, clothing, personal care	$	$	%	$
Vacation, leisure, sports, hobby	$	$	%	$
Fees, bank charges	$	$	%	$
All other expenses	$	$	%	$
State and federal income taxes	$	$	%	$
Totals	$	$	%	$

CASE IN POINT

John and Molly have tracked all expenses for the past two months. They summarized their expenses and discovered that $2,100 is currently being spent on all housing costs, including mortgage, insurance, property taxes, and maintenance. This is roughly 60% of their total expenses monthly. They also spend $670 on groceries and $310 on their cell phones, electricity, and internet, and in total, their monthly expenses are $3,490 per month. After examining their budget closely, they found an additional $300 that could be added to their net cash flow (if they can stick to the budget). Figure 8.6 shows the completed expense budget.

What I Spend Each Day			
Expenses	*Actual*	*Budget*	*Target* Δ
Housing	$2,100	$2,100	$0
Groceries	$670	$500	($170)
Utilities/Phone/ Internet	$310	$250	($60)
All others	$410	$340	($70)
Total Expenses	$3,490	$3,190	($300)

Figure 8.6   Summary (Roll-up) Expense Budget.

In this example, $300 can be freed up to contribute towards other mindful goals and intentions.

Mindful Money Allocation

Now that we know how much we spend and how much we *want* to spend, we have taken care of one of the four money buckets. Now, we can turn to the other areas: investing, saving, and giving.

Using the worksheets, what percent of your total income was spent (in the most recent period or in total)? What percent does that leave you to be generous, to invest with, or to save? There are no magic formulas for getting wealthy, but I recommend that no more than 60% of your cash flows are in the *spending* category. Lower is better. Generally, the less you spend, the more you can grow your money through investments, as well as become more generous.

There are some basic *heuristics* (or shortcuts or guidelines) that the financial industry uses but remember these are just guides and are not specific to your own situation and stage of wealth. The further you are along in age and work, the greater the percent for retirement, as an example. In addition:

- No more than 50% of your total disposable income should be allocated to your household expenses, transportation, food, and other living expenses.
- Lenders often look for housing ratios in which less than 28% of your monthly gross income consists of housing payments (28%), including taxes, insurance, and mortgage or rent.
- Housing (28%) and other consumer debt payments should not exceed 36% in total.
- Most advisers recommend at least 15%–25% of your disposable income should be used for (1) investing, (2) savings, and/or (3) paying down all debts.
- Churches suggest that you tithe or contribute upwards of 10% of what you earn towards charitable or non-profit organizations.

See how these guidelines can be a little confusing? They don't offer a clear path forward, partially because everybody is different ages, risk profiles, needs, and goals.

A general guideline I recommend is this simple formula: **60-15-15-10** (60% spending, 15% investing, 15% retirement, 10% giving). This needs to be modified based on your specific goals and circumstances, of course, but it's a heuristic. If you are more (or less) generous, increase that final percentage up (or down) accordingly. If you have plans of retiring early, you will increase those contributions. If you want to save for college, you need to put more into investments.

You need to focus carefully on this financial allocation. This is the one of the clues to wealth development based on your financial goals. Start by estimating from your expenses about how much you currently "spend" and put that percentage into the model shown in Table 8.4. Then allocate percentages for each of the other three categories. Ask yourself how much you want to "give" to charity, churches, or others as a percent of your total paycheck. How much can you afford to invest? The result will provide estimates of the

Table 8.4 Sample Money Allocation

Allocations	% of Total	Total $
Save	15%	$330
Invest	15%	$330
Spend (including taxes)	60%	$1,320
Give	10%	$220
Specific goal contribution?	*%?*	*$?*
Totals	**100%**	**$2,200**

maximum amount of money you can make by financial decision category. Let's assume you earn $2,200 per month in total from all sources and want to save 15%, invest another 15%, and give 10%; you have 60% available for the monthly expenditures. A total of $1,320 would be the target maximum for the spending budget. Each month, you need to compare your actual spending against this figure to see how it varies over time. You also need to include any additional money to be set aside specifically for your financial goals, that are not in the savings, investment, or giving components. See Table 8.4 for an example of how this works.

This allocation needs to be adjusted as you age and progress. You generally should have a higher percentage in retirement and investing as you age and might have a higher mix towards spending early on in your career. I will repeat the one word of advice which is so vital: start early. If you are young, any small amount you save or invest today will be worth a lot of money later on.

CASE IN POINT

John and Molly together bring home approximately $4,000 per month after taxes. They also sell merchandise on the internet and make about $100 per month, and they receive a $50 dividend check from an energy stock they invested in. Together their total cash inflow is $4,150 per month. They spend an average of $3,490 (or 84% of their net inflows), which yields a $660 per month net disposable income. But if they can stick with their target budget (of $3,190), they will increase this to $960 per month, which can be used towards their goals and increase their wealth.

Personal Balance Sheet

The second most important document that everybody must have (besides the budget) is a personal balance sheet. A *balance sheet* is a summary of what you **own** and what you **owe**, either individually or as a joint couple. If you are married and file taxes jointly, prepare a joint balance sheet. From an account perspective, the balance sheet is the current market value of your assets minus all liabilities (obligations). This results in your "net worth." Net worth is the single most important number for measuring personal wealth.

Mindful Practice 25   Always maintain assets > liabilities.

Don't get too discouraged if your assets are currently less than your liabilities. This is your starting point. Often students or young people who have incurred student loans for education have a negative net worth (or debts > assets). This is normal, but that said, it needs to be a short-term phenomenon. You must strive to make your first financial goal to reverse a negative financial net worth.

The balance sheet is the instrument that allows you to measure the change in your wealth over time. Worth is equal to wealth. All assets should be measured as of the specific date listed, and most are recorded at the current market value. Market value is the price at which you could obtain from a willing buyer if you were to sell them today. For instance, a car or house should be recorded as an asset, at a value equal to what you could get for it if you were to sell it today.

A balance sheet represents your net worth as of a specific date and time. For a balance sheet to be useful, you should monitor changes in the net worth routinely, ideally every month or every three months. The results should be graphically maintained so that you can visually see the changes over time. Our brains have a tendency to understand patterns better when we see them graphically, and this also serves to maintain a clear sense of memory of facts. Our memory recall bias (discussed in Chapter 2) serves to distort our perceptions of facts based on what we selectively recall. When these facts are written down in spreadsheets and viewed graphically, we are much more likely to understand and be able to act on these patterns.

Know Your Numbers

If you want to really make improvements in the momentum-building stages, keep track of your **ESpN**. **E** represents your total value of the equity, or net worth. If you have $75,000 in assets and $62,000 in debts combined, your equity would be $13,000. Aim for increased equity every time. **Sp** represents the spending percentage of the total money coming in. If you earn $5,000 per month and spend $4,000, your

ESpN

E = Equity ($)

Sp = Spending ratio (%)

N = Net cash flow ($)

Sp ratio would be 80%. Aim for less than 60% on this. **N** represents the net cash flow, or reserve, left monthly. Take the difference between money coming in and total money going out, and that provides you with a net cash flow monthly. If you make $5,000 but spend $4,900, you are left with net cash flow of $100 monthly for more mindful money allocation (saving, investing, and giving).

Set a target for the value of your monthly reserve. Target increases in your net worth quarterly. Look to reduce your spending percentage over time.

Just as your physician wants you to remember your body's key numbers (e.g., blood pressure, heart rate) your financial advisor would be ecstatic to know that you have these financial numbers committed to memory! Remember, ESpN.

Financial Gaps in the Reserve

It is common to find households in which the goals and current lifestyle require spending all of the net cash flow with nothing left to invest, save, or give. If you are working in a position that pays near the federal minimum wage, which is currently $7.25 per hour, you would be making approximately $15,000 per year before taxes. This makes money choices even harder. There are times when you must add cash inflows (make more money). There are also times you just need to cut costs.

Based on your needs and goals, you may (1) take additional jobs, find a new one, get a side hustle or (2) completely restructure your day-to-day expenses. Figure 8.7 outlines a flowchart which you can use to identify the logical gaps in your reserves. Follow it through based on your specific scenario. Some of it refers to concepts discussed in Chapter 9 on financial sequencing. See where your problem lies in this figure.

A combination of both bringing in more money and reducing expenditures is usually required to fill financial gaps.

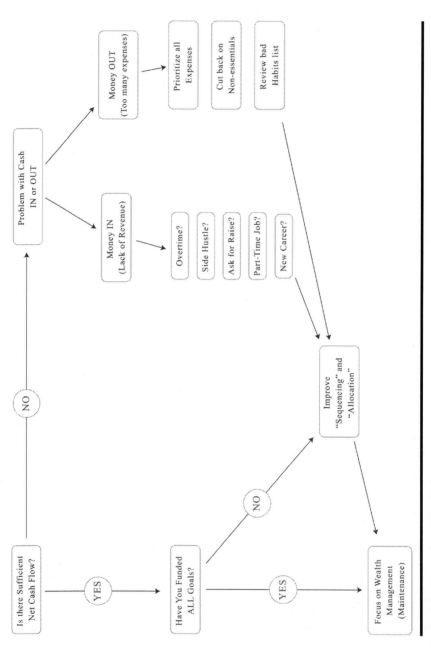

Figure 8.7 Money Flowchart.

Strategies for Getting Focused

In order to get out of this step, you will need to continue to stay focused. Build the initial financial plan, with goals, budget, and net worth statement. Think about this in terms of taking small steps, one day at a time. You won't get there overnight. Here are some specific recommendations for moving on.

1. **Cost cutting.** Based on the detail budget you created earlier, identify five areas that where can save at least $5 per week. Examine areas such as cell phone contracts, expenses eating out at fast food or drinks at restaurants, and even pet food. Definitely track all of your mobile subscriptions. These add up quite quickly. Look through all areas of the expenses you tracked for the past few months. Even small savings from reducing five streaming services could add up to $50 saved per month or $600 per year—that is a good start for building your emergency reserves. You will likely find significantly more than this though since the process tends to uncover spending patterns you did not even realize.

2. **Always pay yourself first.** At this stage, you are re-training your brain to make better choices. One way to do this is to consistently think about paying yourself first. This means, for example, to think about your future before spending money. Think about where you want your key numbers (ESpN). How would these have to change? Begin using automatic deductions for investing and savings directly from your paycheck immediately when it gets deposited. Before you start paying your bills, be sure that you have set up an automatic payment schedule that transfers money out of your checking account into a separate account, such as a money market fund. Focus on your retirement contributions as well. Automate these transfers or withdrawals so the money is not visible in your checking account. This automatic process will help ensure you make necessary contributions in these areas before spending it on other areas.

3. **Generate extra income.** Although you might already have a full-time job, some just do not afford you the ability to pay your bills and achieve the rest of the wealth equation (for savings, investments, and retirement). A second part-time job (or "side hustle") might be necessary at this stage. In addition, think of creative ways you could sell any items that you don't currently use. People often sell their used technology, furniture, and even clothing on sites such as eBay or Facebook Marketplace. Small incremental choices like this can help you to generate the funds to start your savings.

4. **Build cash reserves.** Accumulate money from expense reductions in a money market account at your savings institution. We typically aim for somewhere around three months of cash reserves, which is a simple

heuristic. It really comes down to this—how comfortable would you be today if you lost all sources of income? How long could you survive without some drastic change? Generally, if you are single, you would add more to the reserves, and if you are married and both spouses work, you would have a slightly lower cash reserve. To calculate this, simply add up all of your fixed (those you must pay each month, such as rent or a mortgage) and variable (things like food and gasoline). Add up all of your expenses for a month and multiple by 3. That should be your initial goal for cash reserves. If this sounds overwhelming, just remember to start small. Add in any incremental money you receive into this reserve.

5. **Know your numbers.** It is important to know the primary numbers in your personal finance. Remember ESpN: equity (E), spending ratio (SP), net (N) cash flow monthly. These three numbers are very important. Go back through the last 2–3 months if you can to get good historical data for these figures or start today and document all expenses for the next few months.

6. **Start small.** Don't get easily overwhelmed. Just start small. Open a money market bank account if you don't already have one. Open an investment account online as well (or in person if you prefer), but the online account creations are usually fast and easy. Appendix B has some resources to consider looking at, and the major firms such as Charles Schwab, Fidelity, Vanguard, and T. Rowe Price are all reliable and have excellent tools. Start small by opening an account based on your risk profiles.

Table 8.5 summarizes each of the major points outlined in this chapter.

Table 8.5   Typical Characteristics Found in Step 4 of the Mindful Money Model

Summary	Get Specific
Overall financial profile	Focus on plan development
Money mindset	Moving towards action bias; streamlining; starting to get clear about priorities and vision
Decision style	Informed; tend to use heuristics
Key strategies	Develop budget; know your three key numbers (equity, spend %, net cash flow)
Financial system	Use of apps and software to help organize, track, and optimize; begin to work with a coach or advisor
Current behavioral bias	Recall bias

Take Away

- As we move through the quest for wealth, we must understand our numbers.
- A budget is the most basic instrument necessary to capture historical expenses and to target future spending levels.
- ESpN represents your equity, spending ratio, and net cash flow as of a specific date.
- A mindful allocation of your total money flows should be developed in context to your financial goals.
- An allocation of 60-15-15-10 (60% spending, 15% investing, 15% retirement, 10% giving) is a good starting point until you have carefully identified your goal-specific allocations.
- Identify creative ways to cut costs and improve cash inflows to advance to the next step of wealth.

Key Terms

balance sheet, budget, defensive, ESpN, financial planning, goals, heuristics, intention, mobilizing, monetize, offensive, visioning, why

Chapter 9

Step 5 — Get Momentum

"My wealth has come from a combination of living in America, some lucky genes, and compound interest."

Warren Buffett

The consequence of replacing negative financial habits and making solid money management choices over time will only improve your financial health. First, develop the plan and goals and then stick to them. If you have budgeted $400 per month in food and groceries, then you need to stay on track and spend less than that amount. If your financial plan entails purchasing life insurance, you buy it and keep it. Same with your investment plans. Executing goals and objectives is just as important as developing them in the first place. In the previous chapter, we discussed visioning and mobilizing, the first two activities in planning. This chapter aims to describe sequencing and monitoring, the previous two activities. We will describe concrete strategies for debt management and a financial pyramid that helps to sequence your financial moves.

Momentum

Momentum is that energy or force which keeps you going and is necessary to overcome financial inertia—our behavioral tendency to maintain the status quo. Like a roller coaster, momentum requires four components: initial propulsion, the help of gravity, direction, and time to pick up speed. Same with financial momentum. Start early, save often, head in the right direction, and allow time work in your favor.

With a roller coaster, the initial propulsion is the force which moves the object. With finances, your propulsion is how early you started saving and how much. The more you save early on, the more momentum you will have. Roller coasters also rely on gravity. Gravity helps to speed up the coaster as it races down so that when it turns up, it has sufficient force. With money, gravity is your consistency, and your discipline to keep going over time. Gravity involves not taking out money from retirement and investments so you can use that to build further wealth. A roller coaster stays directed by tracks that keep it on a path. Your direction in money management is dictated by how often you change course and how frequently you make poor decisions or adopt negative habits. A consistent pattern of money choices will keep you heading in the right direction. Finally, a roller coaster uses time to its advantage. At the beginning of the ride, it can't climb large hills. But, as it maintains its course and gravity, time works to its benefit, and at the end of the ride, it can pick up significant steam to perform loops and take steep curves. Likewise, time is essential to building wealth. You can maximize your wealth by focusing on all four components.

Mindful Practice 26   Maximize financial momentum through propulsion, gravity, direction, and time.

In this step, you should focus on paying down and even eliminating all consumer and housing debt. You will work on accurately sequencing your financial activities, paying, investing, and savings in a specific order that yields the most significant economic benefit. Most people also start to rely on outside financial advisors, given the intricacies of this stage. You will need to become hyper-focused on achieving financial goals, and it becomes essential to track and monitor your progress over time. The use of software or automatic expense tracking tools—such as Quicken, Mint, or the Ramsey Every Dollar app—are often used to help monitor budgets, bills, and investments. It pays off to automate your financial management in terms of efficiency and effectiveness later on. It requires a little more work on the front end, but it is worth it.

Most people in this stage see a lot of opportunities and choices that they did not know existed. To keep the momentum going, it is vital to continue to practice the long-term discipline learned in the previous stages. We also have behavioral biases that are very common in stage 4, and these can also derail you.

One of those is the *illusion of control*, when you perceive that you are more in control of things than you are. We see this all the time when you watch sports and see basketball players attempting challenging shots, assuming they will fall in because they think they are superstars and infallible. You also might have an *overconfidence bias*, in which you are overly optimistic and might result in riskier choices. This bias might show up when the stock market has been going up for a few months or years, and it seems like things can't possibly go wrong. Either the illusion of control or *overconfidence bias* may be problematic because you often think you have more control than you do over certain events, such as changes in the stock market or even your employment. It's easy to get lured into a state of emotional and behavioral safety. To achieve wealth, you must remain disciplined and vigilant. One thing we know for sure, especially after the coronavirus pandemic (COVID-19): no one can predict what will happen next.

During this step, we must practice the basics of mindful money management. In the previous chapter, we talked about the first two activities in financial planning (visioning and mobilizing). You've learned how to develop a budget, cash flow statement, and balance sheet. But now the hard part: how do you go about making choices daily? In this section, we discuss some important concepts related to maintaining financial momentum.

Investment Fundamentals

Growth and Compounding

The wealth momentum formula discussed earlier (propulsion, gravity, direction, and time) is based mainly on growth over time. Any amount you set aside in the right type of account, under stable market conditions, and don't withdraw or touch will grow. This is magnified by the *compounding* effect, in which your initial savings are augmented by rates of return or interest, which becomes the new basis for future returns. The more periods of compounding and the higher the returns, the more momentum you will gain. You begin taking advantage of the long-term effects of solid, timely, consistent choices.

Compounding is a simple idea. If you have $10 today and you earned $5 every year going forward, the amount you have in future periods is conceptually based on this simple formula, in which R = return, P = principal balance, g = growth rate, and t = time.

$$R\$ = P + (1 + g)^t$$

If the principal is $10 in year 1 and you grow this plus $5 by the end of the year, you have $15 available to start growing in year 2. So, to maximize this formula, you want high principal values (P) and high growth rates (g) and more time periods. Money management is about maximizing that formula.

In bank accounts, we earn compound growth through interest rates. *Interest* is the amount of money paid for you to keep your cash at a financial institution. Banks use that money to loan out to others, so they pay you a small return as an incentive to maintain your money in their bank in larger and larger amounts. As we mentioned earlier, the incentive paid to you is usually a small percentage rate of return. The current rates hover around 0.1%. Think closely about this number: it is 1/10th of 1%. If it were 1%, and you had $1,000 then annually you would gain $10. But it's 10% × 1% (0.001), so you are earning about $1 on that money per year.

Based on this formula, you are much better off putting money into an investment with higher growth rates, such as a mutual fund or a stock. A *stock* is a small ownership, or share, in a larger corporation or

Risks and returns are directly related.

company. When you own a stock in a company, you become a *shareholder* in the company. A *mutual fund* is when multiple investors pool their money to purchase a portfolio, or diverse collection, of stocks and bonds. With a mutual fund, you typically have small ownership positions in hundreds of different companies, and the price change is reflected in movement by what is called *net asset value (NAV)*. If the NAV, or price of a stock, was $10 last year and $15 this year, in essence, you have made $5 (or 50% on your money; 5/10 × 100). Multiply that by the number of shares you own, and you have your overall return.

Likewise, some stocks pay a dividend. A *dividend* is a payment that a company distributes out of its net profits to its owners or shareholders. If a company makes a profit, it can pay out dividends to reduce its tax liability. Many of the world's leading firms pay pretty significant dividends each year, such as AT&T or ExxonMobil. Some dividends earn 5%–10% each year. That is much better off than a savings account, but it comes with some risk: the stock price could move up or down between periods. We have volatility or instability in pricing. That is the essence of the risk versus return relationship—greater risks produce greater potential returns, while smaller ones yield small returns. Risk and return are directly related.

Look at how changes in the rate of returns impact valuation Table 9.1 shows a table with varying levels of investments and returns over a 10-year period, assuming annual compounding.

Markets and Investments

At one time, most people only purchased individual stocks of corporations that employed them. A *stock* reflects an ownership position (through shares) in the

Table 9.1   Future Value of Investments with Varying Returns After 10 years

Initial Value	1%	5%	10%
$1,000	$1,105	$1,629	$2,594
$15,000	$16,570	$24,433	$38,906
$50,000	$55,231	$81,445	$129,687

company, which allows you to trade on stock markets. Shares of stock are forms of capital, and companies use this mechanism to raise money to fund their business. When the company's performance and outlook increase, the price of that stock should generally rise. If you invest in a single stock, what happens if that stock dramatically falls because of an accounting scandal (like Enron) or another company event? I find that most of us would benefit more from investing in a mutual fund.

As mentioned earlier, a mutual fund is a portfolio of different stocks, or bonds, that are most commonly managed professionally by a financial expert. With a mutual fund, you could select the type of companies you'd like to invest in, the time horizon, the risk profiles, the market sector, and many other things. Mutual funds are sold by the major investment firms but are not traded on an exchange (such as the New York Stock Exchange [NYSE]). Instead, they are redeemed by the broker or firm that offered the fund. Mutual funds are pooled risks—meaning, you aren't just betting your investment on the performance of one single stock. Mutual funds are attractive for most of us for two reasons: (1) you are essentially spreading out the risk and potential for growth from one company (i.e., stock) to multiple companies (i.e., fund), and (2) you are not a full-time professional stock picker!

If you invested it wisely, you might be able to match or even exceed the performance of the stock market overall. A relatively simple choice (with minimal research, lower risks than individual stocks, and good returns) would be to invest in an *index* fund. An index fund is a form of mutual fund that purchases a mix of stocks to mimic the returns of a specific market, such as NYSE or the National Association of Securities Dealers Automated Quotations (Nasdaq). So, if you wanted to earn about what the market as a whole did, you'd purchase an index fund of that market. The Standard and Poor's 500 (S&P 500) index then is a combination of 500 of the largest firms trading on the NYSE that should mimic the returns of the entire market. You can purchase many different types of index funds that could focus on international, small companies, large blue chips, or many others. Mutual funds can be *load* or no-load, which means they might have an upfront cost to purchase these. Think of a load as a commission. You also will be charged an annual operating fee, somewhere between 0.4% and 2.5%. You must carefully look at all these fees before purchasing, as it impacts your overall returns.

If you want to purchase an index fund that is not actively managed and is traded on an exchange, you could opt for an *exchange-traded fund* (ETF). With an ETF, you usually can get an index fund that is much less expensive than a mutual fund because of the passive (electronic) approach to investing. ETFs can have an operating expense ratio of between 0.30% and 0.50%—basically, an annual fee which would cost you about $50 for every $10,000 you invest. There typically are no up-front sales loads on these investments, which makes them very popular.

Regarding stock markets, we commonly talk about the NYSE and Nasdaq, but there are dozens of them. Companies from around the world trade on different markets, including the London Stock Exchange (LSE), Tokyo Stock Exchange (JPX), and Shanghai Stock Exchange (SSE).

Finally, if we generally think the stock market will go down or if we are more conservative in our risk tolerance, we might want to consider bonds. A *bond* is basically a loan (or debt instrument) that a company uses to borrow money from consumers. Bonds generally have a much lower historical rate of return than stocks (equity). Sometimes these bonds are guaranteed by capital (meaning if they fail to repay, you have a right to claim a portion of their assets), but bonds are also unsecured at times (meaning, they are not backed by the assets of the company). Often, people think they are making safe investments, but if the company or municipality that offered the bond goes bankrupt, they could be out of luck.

Importance of Assumptions

When making financial choices, we cannot predict the future, so we must make some assumptions. *Assumptions* are numerical estimates for what we *think*—not hope, not wish, but realistically—will happen in the future. Here are some common things we make assumptions about in money:

- What rate of return might we get on our money?
- What level of *variability* (or *volatility;* unpredictable movement, or change) might we see in any given period?
- How will interest rates move?
- How long would we keep the money in that place?
- What are the opportunity costs (or potential returns we are giving up) by making this choice?

We must make these assumptions, or best guesses, on these types of questions to understand the impact of our choices.

Consider this example. You just received an inheritance of $50,000 today. Examine the assumptions shown in Table 9.2.

Since the historical returns averaged 7.5% and we have no reason to suspect this will be any different going forward, we use that as the future projections. The *beta* (B) reflects the degree of systematic risk for the investment relative to the market in total. This is sometimes called overall market risk. If it's less than 1, it's less risky than the market as a whole, whereas any number greater than 1 is more vulnerable to risk. It could produce greater returns, but it's also more volatile. For simplicity of illustration, I will ignore the uncertainty (or potential variability) in returns, which could have either magnified the gain or reduced it slightly. Using that as your base, you could invest in the market each year you would earn 7.5% of the value, if you don't touch it or remove any money. That way, after year 1, your return would be $50,000 + $3,750 (or $50,000 × 0.075) = $53,750. Keep that balance in there and don't take any withdrawals, and if the market returns 7.5% in the second year, you would get more than just $3,750 in returns because your base is larger now. So, year two would give you $4,031 in returns and a total balance of $57,781. Do this same math over 10 years, and your $50,000 turns into over $103,000. That's a whopping doubling (or technically, 106% return) of your money!

If you choose to save it in the bank savings account, here are your alternative returns: the current interest rate is 0.10% (or 0.001). Your $50,000 would only return you $50 in interest after year one and only $502 for the entire 10 years— safer and less risky but nearly nothing in return. Figure 9.1 shows the effect of compounding.

This is the trade-off we have between savings and investing. Savings is usually less likely to decrease in terms of the *principal* balance (the initial money you

Table 9.2   Investment Assumptions

Historical rate of return, investments	7.5% annually
Beta	1.0
Potential uncertainty or variability	+0.10%
Principal	$50,000
Alternative interest rate	0.10%
Time period	10 years

invested). But it likely won't grow much. Meanwhile, investing has the potential to earn significant returns and growth on top of those returns. What is essential is that you recognize what level of risk you are willing to take on the principal and understand the trade-off in terms of growth.

What we learn from this is two-fold: (1) compounding can be instrumental in building momentum and wealth, and (2) not touching the principal balance is essential to the growth. When you invest, let the money and time work for you.

Of course, we can't forget our risk profile and money personality entirely. We had to overcome fear to get through the first two thresholds in the quest, and one of them requires you to be a little more (or a little less based on your type) open to risk. Consider your investments to be "out of reach"—don't try to constantly re-think them, change them, or withdraw money—unless there is a really good reason! The wealth momentum formula needs time and growth to work in your favor.

---

*Mindful Practice 27   Don't churn
or withdraw invested money.*

Financial Sequencing

Now let's turn back to the financial planning process. We started in Chapter 8 developing your financial vision and goals and then gathering and mobilizing data for your key numbers. Now the third activity of the financial planning process (i.e., visioning, mobilizing, sequencing, monitoring) is all about *sequencing*. Sequencing is correctly ordering our financial moves. What do I mean? Well, if you are drowning in student loan debt, I wouldn't recommend you invest the incremental money (or net cash flows) you receive. You would probably be better off first paying off debt, especially high-interest debt that accumulates. Paying off the debt would also reduce the principal balance and future interested charges on that balance. Compounding works on debt, too—the more obligation you have, the more you will get charged, and it becomes a vicious cycle of paying down your debt on top of debt.

Sequencing suggests that there is a proper order in which to make money choices. Usually, we make choices based on improving our net worth, improving monthly net cash flow, reducing tax liability, and reducing overall debt. We should evaluate each money

For each choice, ask "What move now will improve my wealth?"

The Effect of Compounding Growth

Scenario 1	Year 1	Year 2	Year 3	Year 4	Year 5	Year 6	Year 7	Year 8	Year 9	Year 10
Beginning	$50,000	$53,750	$57,781	$62,115	$66,773	$71,781	$77,165	$82,952	$89,174	$95,862
Percent % Return	7.5%	7.5%	7.5%	7.5%	7.5%	7.5%	7.5%	7.5%	7.5%	7.5%
Money $ Return	$3,750	$4,031	$4,334	$4,659	$5,008	$5,384	$5,787	$6,221	$6,688	$7,190
Ending Balance	$53,750	$57,781	$62,115	$66,773	$71,781	$77,165	$82,952	$89,174	$95,862	$103,052

The Effect of Compounding Growth

Scenario 2	Year 1	Year 2	Year 3	Year 4	Year 5	Year 6	Year 7	Year 8	Year 9	Year 10
Beginning	$50,000	$50,050	$50,100	$50,150	$50,200	$50,251	$50,301	$50,351	$50,401	$50,452
Percent % Return	0.1%	0.1%	0.1%	0.1%	0.1%	0.1%	0.1%	0.1%	0.1%	0.1%
Money $ Return	$50	$50	$50	$50	$50	$50	$50	$50	$50	$50
Ending Balance	$50,050	$50,100	$50,150	$50,200	$50,251	$50,301	$50,351	$50,401	$50,452	$50,502

Figure 9.1   The Effect of Compounding Growth.

move based on its improvement in your key numbers, especially our equity (net worth).

Think about debt as your enemy and attack it with a vengeance. Debt is wrong for so many reasons: it not only hampers your ability to choose something more wealth-building, but debt obligations also tend to grow over time. You might end up making a minimum payment on a credit card that only covers the interest charges accrued that month, so you might never make progress on debt reduction. I have seen many people only making the minimum required payments and never begin to reduce the principal balance they owe. Debt is destructive to wealth.

Armed with your three key numbers (remember ESpN; equity, spending %, and net cash flow), you now have the critical pieces of information necessary to implement your financial plan. You can begin tackling your liabilities and building your wealth. As shown previously in the John and Molly case in Chapter 8, the couple currently has an opportunity to build their wealth by over $960 per month if they stick to a plan. Now how should they deploy that to create the most wealth? Also, what if you didn't have any extra money left over after reviewing your budget and your current cash flow? What then? What should you do with your money to make the wisest choices?

The choices with what we can do with any additional money (whether it's $20 per month or $900) are limited to one of the four types of decisions we discussed earlier: we can spend it, save it, invest it, or give it away. Which one of these we choose to do will determine our path towards wealth. Like the food pyramid, I developed a financial pyramid to conceptualize the sequence of financial decisions to attack your debts and build your wealth.

The sequence in which you do things matters. You always have a choice and nearly always two or more alternatives. Consider this example: you have an extra $100 you received for your birthday from your aunt. Let's say you chose to use that to spay $100 off towards credit card debt, which currently has a $2,000 balance. At the end of that month, you still have $1,900 in debt, plus interest due over those 30 days (which would probably generate an additional $24 increase the next month with 15% interest rate if you didn't make any additional purchases). So, alternative 1 produces a result of $1,924 in debt and $0 in cash. Instead, you could have invested that into a savings account (which would earn you about 0.05% currently, or less than $1 in interest income per year, and just a few cents per month). So, alternative 2 would have $2,025 at the end of the month in debt, and $100 in cash.

Or should you put it into a retirement account (alternative 3)? Pay off that new iPhone you bought from T-Mobile (alternative 4)? Which one is the right choice? How do we know which one is the optimal choice? There are of course multiple paths, such as either using your judgement or a more contemplative process that focuses on minimizing debts or maximizing future growth. Of course, one path is not always the best, given the nature of some financial plans, but usually, one approach does have a better overall impact on your financial health.

If you face a complex decision, I recommend using a piece of paper and writing down the options. A *decision tree* is a visual flowchart resembling a tree, which presents the options in front of you and the probability (or likelihood) that a particular outcome or event will result. The decision tree is one way to represent the choice you are facing. Figure 9.2 shows a simple decision tree of this problem.

We could make that a complicated graphic—we could estimate probabilities, cost or returns, and then produced weighted utility (or benefits that will be used to satisfy a consumer's needs) for each event. But again, most of you are not going to do this with most of your daily money choices. Nor do I. It's just not practical. But a simple version of a decision tree can be really good to help you think through your options and their potential payoffs.

We need to internalize the thought process of what goes into the decision so that if we are pressed for time or need a mental shortcut, we are focusing on the correct variables. In nearly all cases, we should be asking all of these questions to make good choices:

- What alternatives or options do I have?
- What are the likelihood of each of those options occurring?
- What are the upside (benefits) and downside (weaknesses) of this approach?
- What level of uncertainty or risk will I face?
- What would be the cost (or return, depending on what you're looking at)?
- What option challenges me or makes me feel secure?
- What would be the final utility or outcome for each of these events?

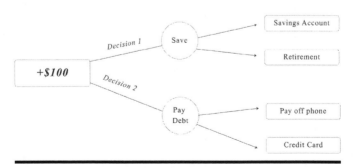

Figure 9.2   Financial Decision Tree.

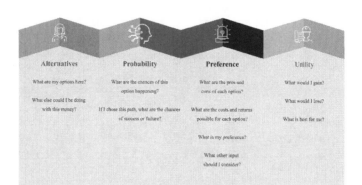

Figure 9.3   Considerations for Financial Choices.

Your infinitely flexible brain has more than enough capacity to ponder those things prior to a decision. Definitely, you must contemplate some factors and questions that will help improve the odds of a satisfactory decision. I categorize these into four groups: alternatives, probabilities, preferences, and utility. Each one of these categories has some questions you should consider when making any choice—definitely any choice which requires significant exposure to your money. I outline these in Figure 9.3. Try to ask yourself those questions any time you are unsure of something. If your aunt left you an inheritance of $1 million versus the $100 earlier, that would require significantly more time and contemplation.

Consider the Impact of Time

To make the decision that best impacts your wealth, you ideally should be considering the impact on your cash flow and balance sheet statement simultaneously. Any positive choice would create an increase in wealth in subsequent periods and free up disposable income. But given the way our brains work, we often just do what is easy or directly in front of us. If we received that $100 right before we went shopping, we might spend it. If we received it while standing in the phone store, we'd likely put that towards the phone. If we just read an article about retirement planning, we would do that.

A more deliberate plan would suggest separating the current moment from the best solution (we call this removing *time dependency*). You bring the decisions to a more conscious level when you think about them and seek out the choice that maximizes your potential for wealth.

To make this more visual, think about your choices in terms of two factors: (1) the potential impact that your choice might have on your overall wealth and (2) the speed and ease with which you can realize that utility. A matrix that presents these two factors is shown in Figure 9.4.

If you were pressed to make a choice today and had to choose between an investment (or purchase) which could make you a lot of money and would take no time to realize this benefits, do that first. That would be the top priority (which I call priority A in the matrix). Choices that have minimal impact on your total wealth and take a long time to realize and might be difficult to do are low priority (priority C). In between are the tough ones. These require some contemplation and possibly a decision tree because either might be good, and they ultimately depend on your situation and where they sit on the axes.

In Figure 9.5, I use the same matrix to show how I would structure major money decisions, assuming additional or incremental dollars. By this I mean if you were given additional funds today to make a decision, which of the four matrix options would you pursue? Keep in mind that these are just general tips, so you still need to consider your own unique risk profiles, financial circumstances, and timelines before making any decisions.

For instance, routine consistent investing and paying off your credit, student, and car debts probably have some of the biggest impacts on your wealth because they are shorter time to benefits. Purchasing a home and maximizing your retirement contributions are really good long-term moves, with a lasting impact on your wealth potential. But given the time frame, they would be a somewhat lower priority. While a wonderful idea for the long-term, buying or

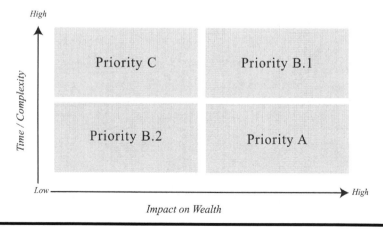

Figure 9.4   Choice Prioritization Matrix.

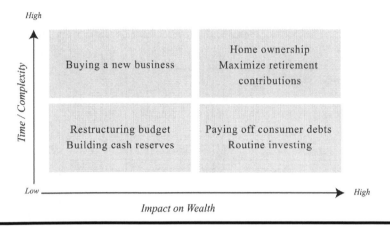

Figure 9.5 Prioritizing Traditional Money Choices.

starting a brand-new business would not immediately have a positive financial impact, plus it would require a lot of complexity and time.

There is not a "right or wrong" answer. We must look for our time horizon and impact on wealth and do a mix of money choices that will improve your portfolio overall and key numbers. Weigh all of these factors when deciding what to do. Figure 9.5 presents some of these options.

CASE IN POINT

Some of us drive around all day to find the cheapest gas per gallon. Nothing wrong with saving money, but you should focus on using your time wisely to maximize value. Consider this example. If gasoline was $0.25 per gallon less expensive at a station all the way across the city (let's say from $2.75/gallon to $2.50), that would be significant, right? Nearly a 10% drop in the price per gallon. There are apps and internet websites devoted to helping you find that specific station, so you spend time researching and driving, plus waiting in line. But step back and do the math on this. If you save $0.25/gallon (and drove the typical 1,200 miles per month with 20 miles per gallon), you would be saving only $15 per month (or $0.50 per day). I am not at all suggesting that you shouldn't save money—look for all ways to save—but weigh the benefits against the costs. If you save 50 centers per day, don't buy an energy drink at the gas station. Spend the same amount of time looking for opportunities to cut more significant ticket items, such as a car you don't need or services you pay for but don't use.

Retirement

A large number of people who eventually become wealthy do so through their retirement savings. Retirement savings is a type of investment set aside for your post-working years. Most companies offer some form of retirement savings, and they are often tax deferred until you actually use the funds. *Tax deferred* refers to postponing the timing of when your federal taxes are due, based not on when you received the funds but when you actually take distributions. Companies offer *qualified* plans—employer-sponsored plans that receive special tax treatment for deductions under the Internal Revenue Service (IRS) code. You might have heard of 401k, 403b, or tax-sheltered annuity. These all are specific types of qualified retirement plans.

There are both defined benefits and defined contribution plans. You should make sure you understand what your retirement plan is at your employer and maximize those contributions. *Defined benefit* plans typically will pay lifetime benefits if you qualify under the requirements of the plan, based on a formula typically comprised of years tenure, average salary, and other factors. *Defined contribution* means that your

> *Maximize your employer sponsored retirement contributions. Tax deferrals magnifies growth.*

employer is setting aside a specific amount of money each pay period, and you will choose the investment and be responsible for any risks and returns. Defined contributions are tax deductible, and accumulated earnings grow tax deferred. Know which retirement plan you have.

You should also consider incorporating both pre-tax and post-tax retirement investing into an *individual retirement account* (IRA). Pre-tax generally refers to your employer deducting pre-tax contributions and transferring that money into a separate investment account held at a financial institution. Your contribution can be tax deductible but be sure to look up the current IRS adjusted gross income requirements, which might limit your deduction. You also save the payroll taxes that you would have paid on that money. If your company doesn't offer that, you could invest into an IRA on your own through a *Roth IRA*—a special form of IRA that accepts after-tax contributions and allows money to grow tax free (with certain income limitations and stipulations). When you go to withdraw the money years later, you will have already paid all of the taxes due, and your money continues to grow tax free.

The traditional and the Roth IRA both have specific IRS guidelines you must follow for deductions to qualify, which you can find on the IRS's website (www.irs.gov).[65] IRAs are good for retirement, but you need to learn more about the options available to you specifically.

To become wealthy, we must mindfully contribute to available retirement plans. The compounding growth effect we discussed earlier is magnified by the tax impact. Since we are not having to pay income taxes on most of these (current federal rates for most people are between 10% and 35%, based on your earnings level) or payroll taxes (for Medicare and Social Security), we are investing in a tax-advantaged way. That marginal tax rate keeps that additional amount of money working for you, until a much later point in time when you are ready to use it. If you make more money today than we would in retirement, you are earning a tax advantage since your income taxes due will be less in those years.

How much do we need to have for retirement? There are many ways people have tried to create heuristics on this. Some of the most popular are these.

1. **The 4% guideline.** This suggests that you plan a retirement goal in which each year you could withdraw up to 4%. So, if you had $1 million set aside for retirement, you would be able to take no more than $40,000 in the first year. This heuristic though has some serious shortcomings. The longevity risk we described earlier could really upset the logic on this calculation.

2. **A percentage of pre-retirement income.** A second way people tend to estimate their retirement needs is to calculate how much you will actually spend in retirement each year. You might not have a house payment for example or as much work-related costs such as transportation. So, people use estimates, such as 75% or 80% of their pre-retirement income. We would then input this number into a financial calculator and estimate how much you will need by the time you retire. I find this to be very imprecise method, since there is such variability in what you might spend over time. When somebody retires, they might spend a lot of money in the first few years while they are traveling, but over time, it substantially decreases (except for healthcare, which will definitely increase).

3. **Rule of 72.** A final heuristic is the rule of 72, which says that 72 divided by the rate of return you are earning will result in the number of years until your money doubles. If you earn 10% on your money, then 72/10 = 7.2 years. In essence, you double your money ever 7 years. If you earn 6%, it will take 12 years to double your money. This heuristic is helpful to get a general idea of the future value of a retirement asset, despite having limitations in its simplicity.

Keep in mind that these approaches are heuristics. I would look at your retirement needs in various ways to get different perspectives on what you really need at retirement. Prioritize maximizing your retirement contributions while you still can during your working years to take advantage of the tax deferrals and compounding.

Financial Pyramid

Conceptually, I hope this makes sense. I am sure at first glance it might seem overwhelming. But it's not difficult! Remember, small steps and choices make a huge impact. You want to make choices that are more likely to increase your wealth (financial health) over the long run, taking into account some risks, costs, complexity, and time. But again, the difficulty is in the application. To help make this much clearer, I created a financial pyramid which presents an optimal sequence (under most circumstances) of when to make some of the most common money management decisions. Use this financial pyramid as a heuristic to guide you if you don't have the time or patience to develop your own decision tree or matrix.

The pyramid is structured to show decisions on the base (lower) level that you should make first. These serve as the foundation to what comes next. All are necessary to create wealth. Everything we have discussed in the book is essential, of course, but the pyramid will help you sequence these activities. It's a decision of "when," not "if," you do these strategies!

They are also loosely tied to the stages of wealth; the base level operates in steps 1–3, while the middle involves steps 4 and 5. The very top level is step 6, where you've made it to your version of wealth, and you need to sustain it. You work your way through the bottom, left to right, and then up the pyramid as you attack each of the areas. Figure 9.6 shows the financial pyramid, which we will discuss in detail.

Fundamental Financial Moves

We will start with the fundamental decisions that you must start to do with your money, assuming you have gotten clear about your money mindset and have become specific with your goals.

1. Build a Cash Emergency Account

The sequence should involve first developing emergency cash reserves. Most financial planners suggest three to six months of cash reserves. If this sounds overwhelming, start by building a habit of small contributions first. If you make $3,000 per month and just started a full-time job at age 23, start by putting aside $25 or $50 per paycheck into a separate money market account. As you build experience doing this, the number needs to be gradually increased. The goal of having three to six months of cash in an emergency reserve account would equal $9,000 to $18,000. That may sound like a lot, but if you break it

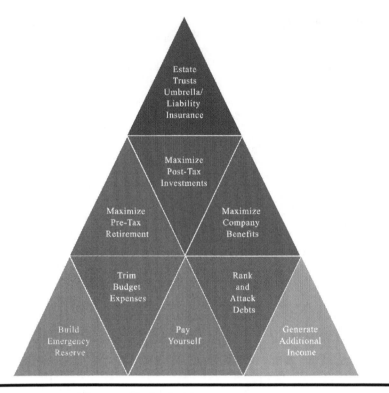

Figure 9.6 Financial Pyramid of Priorities.

down into smaller chunks, you will find that this can be accomplished fairly quickly. I recommend putting your money into a very conservative, risk-free account such as a money market savings account at your local savings institution. Alternately, you could seek out a higher-yield interest accounts which pays four to five times the interest rate of the national bank chains.

2. *Follow Your Budget and Trim Expenses*

After you have built your emergency reserve account, you need to follow the target budget. Monitoring your ongoing expenses will help you to stay on track. In order to meet the target, you will need to trim your expenses (and possibly get a second job to raise additional cash inflows). Trimming expenses can range from large items taken out of your budget to smaller ones. Here are some practical tips to consider that many people can achieve relatively painless:

Identify any accounts that charge monthly fees without providing any service. For example, your bank accounts might be charging you monthly if your balance is too low. Your goal is to eliminate all fees from your budget—don't pay any late fees, overdraft charges, or bank service charges. If you do, find a different institution.

- Identify the top spending areas that are not fixed costs per month and work first on those categories (such as dining out, groceries, and personal items).
- Eliminate phone or TV subscriptions which you don't use. Any streaming service that you haven't used in more than a month should be eliminated.
- Look at items that you haven't negotiated or considered in a while. This includes your electricity bill. In many parts of the country, there are options for natural gas, oil, or electricity. Compare rates and see if you can getter better pricing elsewhere.

3. Pay Yourself First

We mentioned this earlier, but the concept of making your goals the highest priority is one of the most important behavioral principles in money management. You pay yourself first by using your allocation strategy to fund your goals immediately. Rather than waiting and seeing how much money is left at the end of the month to invest, you invest first a consistent monthly amount and then spend the remainder. It's a flipped strategy. For example, utilize automatic transfers out of your bank account immediately once you are paid each period into a separate investment or retirement account. Depending on the calculation for your cash reserves and other goals, this amount needs to be pre-determined. Once you have the decided upon an amount, transfer this money into that separate account. I strongly recommend the use of an index fund or general growth-based mutual fund. Remember from our earlier definition, an index fund is a mutual fund, or compilation of multiple stocks and assets, that seeks to match the overall return of an entire exchange market of stocks. The Standard and Poor's 500 and the Dow Jones Industrial Average have multiple index funds from a variety of firms that you can invest in if you have a good risk profile. If you are more conservative and worried about losing money, there are hundreds of other more conservative mutual funds you can consider.

4. Rank and Attack Debts

We talked about this earlier but ranking and attacking your debts is critical. Your high-interest debt such as credit cards, revolving store accounts, and student loans have multiple finance charges. With the average American having a balance of over $6,000 and an average interest rate of 18%, the interest charges alone annually would be over $1,100—or $100 extra per month. Remember that charges and fees have no role in wealth. You are simply increasing your expenses, without any change in net worth.

There are three basic approaches to debt management. One of these must be part of your financial plan. They all start with ranking debts by balance due, interest rate being charged, and/or length of time the debt is due. You use the same tracking tools we discussed previously. Outline all of the liabilities (people and firms you owe money to), as well the current balance and interest rates. Once you have them organized, you could manage them either by overall balance or by interest rate. Look at Figure 9.7. In this example, if you chose the debt snowball you would target the store credit account first followed by student loan. In the avalanche approach, you'd choose the store credit followed by credit cards (in this example).

1. **Debt avalanche.** A debt avalanche refers to a steep and sudden slope. A *debt avalanche* is a rapid and overwhelming quantity of debt being accrued monthly, through interest or finance charges. This strategy suggests you pay the debts off first that have the highest interest rate. You would make minimum required payment, to stay fully in compliance with your other lenders, and utilize all available funds in your spending category to pay down these debts first. Start by ranking all of your debts (similar to Figure 9.7 but by annual percentage rate) and work on paying the most

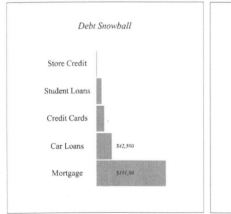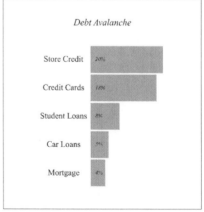

Figure 9.7   Debt Strategies.

money towards the one with the highest overall interest rate. Once that is paid off, move to the debt with the next highest interest rate.

2. **Debt snowball.** A *debt snowball* strategy pays off the debts that are the smallest first and makes minimum payments on all other accounts. This way, you can build some positive momentum to attack the larger items. Once you pay off the smallest obligation, move on to the next smallest until you have paid them all off.

3. **Debt consolidation.** In this case, you consolidate or merge all of your debts into one. Some people have tried to use their house equity to do this, while others receive a debt consolidation loan that effectively transfers all the balance from the other accounts into one, so you are making payments now on only one account. This is particularly useful when families have found themselves with balances on multiple credit cards, have two or three student loans, and are having trouble keeping up with minimum payments on all accounts.

I suggest you use one of the first two and avoid consolidation loans due to additional fees that sometimes are attached to them. If you have one account that is extremely high in interest rates while others are lower, I recommend using the avalanche approach. From the numbers perspective, the avalanche is probably the wisest financial move. From a behavioral perspective, I'd go with the snowball. You will feel a sense of accomplishment a lot faster!

5. Generate Additional Income

Sometimes the problem with insufficient disposable income is that we spend too much. Other times, we just don't earn enough to cover the lifestyle we are living. Most of the time, we need to do better in all areas. If you find that you need additional income to meet the guidelines suggested earlier, then part-time jobs in the evening or "side hustles" can be used to supplement your income. There are multiple ways to generate extra income from driving for Uber or a food delivery service to starting a small online store to sell your used technology.

6. Maximize Company and Government Benefits, Retirement, and Investing

Once you have taken care of all the items on the bottom of the financial pyramid, you're ready to focus on maximizing all investment, retirement, and other company benefits that might be due to you. If you are self-employed, this means utilizing health savings accounts (HSA) with a high deductible health plan or a simplified employee pension plan. If you are employed, look for any matching on retirements and 401k profit-sharing plans. A *match* represents the percent that your company will put into a plan, as a percentage of what you contribute. Many plans default to a 100% match on your first 3% of salary deferrals. You must fully maximize the match percentage—if the company will contribute 50% of the first 6% of your income put into a plan, you need to contribute all 6%. Let me give a simple example. Assuming you made $50,000 gross, you would contribute a percentage (or $3,000) per year into a retirement account. The company would match that with $1,500 (or 50% of your contributions), which basically increases your net worth by $1,500 for no additional effort. Taking advantage of the match is basically free money to you, and it's how you gain momentum.

Other often overlooked options include taking advantage of all employer benefits, even small ones such as wellness, fitness, and cell phone discounts. Continue to focus on regularly investing your net cash flows (or reserves). Utilize a monthly *dollar-cost averaging* approach, which basically means to just keep investing on a routine basis, no matter if the market goes up or down. Dollar cost averaging slits your investments into regular periods to avoid the volatility in the market. Getting used to these as routine contributions helps your brain overcome the temptation to alter them and use that money for other purposes.

There are excellent government programs, such as Medicare and Social Security, for those who qualify. If you are approaching the age of 65, be sure you to sign up for Medicare. Medicare provides government-sponsored healthcare, which is essential for most people after they lose their company-provided health-care insurance. There are multiple parts which can be confusing. Medicare Part A covers all the hospital costs if you were admitted into a facility. Part B pays for the physician visits but not the hospital. Part C is a supplemental plan offered by a third part that you might consider instead of A and B. Part D is prescription medication coverage. You must enroll to receive Medicare, and there is only one time per year to enroll: mid-October of every year for approximately six to seven weeks. Don't miss the enrollment deadline during the year you turn 65 years old.

Also, be sure to check your Social Security benefits at www.ssa.gov and weigh the benefits of taking it as early as age 62 versus postponing to retirement age or beyond. There are numerous financial calculators that can help you compare the monthly and cumulative impact. You will receive more money per month in benefits when you delay taking benefits after your full retirement age (which generally is either 66 or 67 years, depending on your birth year). You can enroll for both Medicare and Social Security in one online application.

At the top of the pyramid, the focus is on maintaining wealth. We typically have all our debts paid, and we need to focus on maintaining liability insurance and working on estates and trusts. We cover these additional subjects in Chapter 10.

Decision Strategies

This stage can be a long one and may take years or even decades. Following are summary strategies for making better choices and moving on to the next step towards wealth.

1. **Choose consistency.** While it is possible to save significant sums of money elsewhere, most people will never achieve wealth if they don't invest in the stock market. I don't personally recommend most individual stocks due to the risk of isolated stocks. Based on your risk profile, you might consider setting aside money in a mutual fund that matches your risk style and investment horizon. Mutual funds allow for investments in multiple stocks, bonds, or fixed income securities while distributing potential risks and returns across multiple companies. Mutual funds are the simplest way to get in the market. Based on historical performance, mutual funds that are weighted heavier in equities (stocks) tend to outperform those that invest in bonds or fixed securities, but the choice needs to be based on your expected returns and risk tolerance.
2. **Maximize company benefits and retirement contributions.** If your company pays a match percentage for a 401k, profit-sharing, or other retirement plans, you should invest at least that same percentage. Consider a traditional or Roth IRA. At this stage, you should be maximizing your retirement contributions (currently in 2021 at $19,500 per year) on a pre-tax basis. If your company provides a 3% match, invest at least 100% of that figure and gradually move up to the highest amount possible. If there are company benefits, such as gym memberships or cell phone discount plans, be sure to find them and utilize all company benefits. You will be surprised how much money you can save each month this way.
3. **Get rid of debt.** Avoid the temptation of becoming comfortable with debt. It's very easy to get used to a monthly car payment, student loan, or other obligation. Debt helps you to afford things that you might not be able to do otherwise (we call that leverage). But in personal finance, debt is destructive to building wealth. To work your way out of debt, adopt one of the strategies for paying off your outstanding obligations: debt avalanche, debt snowball, or debt consolidation. To start, write down all debts, including home mortgage, credit cards, student loans, automobile loans, personal loans, and any debts to family members or others. List the balances, current interest rate percentage annually, and type of debt. We discuss these more in the subsequent chapter.
4. **Don't try to time the market.** Many people try to figure out when the market will go down, thus triggering them to buy. Then when it's down,

they question whether it will go down further. And finally, as the prices increase well above where it once was, the investor is looking to wait. This wait-and-see approach is not a good strategy. Very few people get wealthy by timing the market but rather utilize a more disciplined approach such as dollar-cost averaging, which we will discuss in the subsequent chapter.

5. **Don't become a stock picker.** There are thousands of people with advanced training, research, tools, and computers that are looking for the best ways to maximize *alpha* (or excess returns for a stock relative to their risk) over a particular benchmark or the entire market. Even with all their resources, most professional analysts cannot over-perform the general market in the long run. Leave that to the professionals and primarily invest in mutual funds and index funds.

Table 9.3 summarizes the characteristics associated with step 5.

Take Away

- Wealth accumulates over time through a series of properly sequenced and persistent financial moves.
- Maximize all contributions when you can receive a company match for those funds.

Table 9.3   Summary of Step 5

Summary	Get Momentum
	Implementing all aspects of your financial plan
Overall financial profile	Investment and retirement accounts are established; working through the financial pyramid; monitoring key numbers (i.e., ESpN)
Money mindset	More analytically driven; biased towards action
Decision style	Knowledgeable; analytical
Key strategies	Use of wealth momentum formula (propulsion, gravity, direction, time); financial pyramid and sequencing
Financial system	Organized; collaborative with outside assistance
Current behavioral bias	Illusion of control, overconfidence bias

- Keep in mind the powerful effect of compounding growth, which makes your money work for you over time. Start early.
- Work through your debt systematically via one of three debt strategies, including avalanche, snowball, and consolidation.
- Consider the use of decision trees to map out your options and alternatives.
- Using more complex thinking, you can organize alternatives based on probability, preferences, and utility.
- There is a preferred sequence of money choices you should make based on your current financial position. Sequencing through the financial pyramid can help to prioritize your money moves based on time and wealth.

Key Terms

alpha, assumption, beta, bond, compounding, debt avalanche, debt snowball, decision tree, defined benefit, defined contribution, dividend, dollar-cost averaging, equity, exchange-traded fund, financial pyramid, illusion of control, index fund, individual retirement account (IRA), interest, load, match, mutual fund, overconfidence bias, principal, qualified plan, Roth IRA, sequencing, stock, systematic risk, tax-deferred, time-dependency, utility, variability, volatility

CROSSING THE BRIDGE OF PERSEVERANCE

"Our intention creates our reality."

Wayne Dyer

Our quest for wealth is nearly complete. But first, we must pass over the bridge of perseverance, where you fortify your system of making mindful choices. If you can persevere, wealth is in sight! Chapter 10 discusses the final step in our quest and provides multiple tools and practices for managing wealth. Chapter 11 offers recommendations and strategies for how to improve daily choices. Chapter 12 wraps up with a summary of all the Mindful Money Practices outlined throughout the book.

DOI: 10.4324/9781003231844-12

Chapter 10

Get Wealthy

"Wealth is just consistency. I don't want to be rich. I want to be wealthy"

Quavo

You have done it! You have worked your way to the final step in the quest towards wealth. Here you are looking to continue to grow and sustain your resources, also called wealth management. You might not yet feel wealthy, but you will get there if you are consistently making wise choices. You are achieving your financial goals.

At this point, you should be focusing on the six areas of wealth shown in Figure 10.1. Some of these we have already talked about and others we will here briefly in this chapter.

Insurance & Risk
Term life, auto, homeowners, health, umbrella, business

Tax Planning
Federal income, state income, property

Investments
Stocks, bonds, mutual funds portfolio management

Estates and Trusts
Wills, power of attorney, trust documents, estate plans

Retirement
Pensions, 401k, 403b, social Security

Education Planning
College financial aid, student loans, education needs assessments

Figure 10.1 Components of Wealth Management Planning.

DOI: 10.4324/9781003231844-13

Critical here are the activities at the top of the financial pyramid we showed in the previous chapter, including monitoring all your accounts, developing estate and trust plans, and maintaining full liability insurance.

Estate Planning Fundamentals

In a recent Charles Schwab survey, investors were asked to describe the dollar threshold required to be considered wealthy—the average response answer was $1.9 million in combined savings and investments.[66] That sounds like an enormous sum of money to most people. Of course, there are a couple of significant issues with those survey results. First, they surveyed a hand-picked group of their own customers, who were all probably active and interested investors, not the typical American. Second, we can't rely on any magic number. Any number is just a guide to help focus your direction since there is no universal number for the optimal size of your financial worth (or estate).

All of us have an estate, no matter what step of wealth. An *estate* is the total of all your equity in your accumulated assets. Your estate includes your house, car, investments, retirement, and any other objects you own. Estates also must consider the impact of any obligations you owe on those assets—if you have any loans, liens, or debts against your assets, as well as any taxes that are due. Therefore, our *estate plans* are the documents we use to manage the ongoing protection and eventual distribution of your net worth at some point in the future.

I am not an attorney, so I will present the fundamental concepts in estate planning. By the time you get to this step, you will have acquired a fair amount of assets. You must protect your estate so you can use it or give it away as you choose. Did you know that if you died without a will, the state you live in would be responsible for divvying up your assets? A *will* is a legal document that provides instructions on who and how to distribute certain assets. A will can be used to gift your car or jewelry for example. And if you don't have a will—the county and state you reside in will decide for you! A will is essential for everyone.

In your will, an executor must be named. An *executor* is the person (or institution) you name in a will to manage the distribution of your assets after your death. An executor can be your spouse or child, a friend, or an attorney, or it could be a financial organization. You should carefully determine who that person should be. People often pick a person close to them

> **Routinely communicate your intentions to beneficiaries and executors while you can.**

instead of someone who can remain independent who is good with finances or at least understands legal and financial processes. That is a mistake; pick somebody that can pay your bills and take care of all the necessary arrangements you had planned for. It is essential to understand that executors cannot change your wishes—the will outlines what they are required by law to do, and they distribute your assets accordingly.

But wills do not cover all of your estate. Something important to consider is that a will is only useful for assets that do not pass by contract or law. What that means in practical terms is that if somewhere you have identified a successor of your assets legally, that asset will likely bypass your will. If you have a mutual fund or stock, for example, you should instead designate a beneficiary because these distribute more efficiently. A *beneficiary* is the person who receives the rights to that asset after you die. To be proactive, each account should have its own beneficiary designations, so be sure to check all your bank accounts, investments, and retirement accounts to ensure that you have the person you intend to receive these funds listed as beneficiary. If you don't have a beneficiary listed yet, I would recommend you do so immediately. If you were to die with no beneficiary, then your will would determine how the assets are divided. The same goes for bank accounts or certificates of deposit. Typically, you list a beneficiary or successor who would receive those by contract or law rather than by will. So don't rely exclusively on your will.

You should also have a *power of attorney (POA)*. A POA is a legal document that assigns someone else to have authority over making specific kinds of decisions if you become unable to perform certain duties. A POA can be durable, which is sustained in case you are incapacitated, or it can be limited, which is based on time or a specific condition. One example of a limited POA is a medical POA, which grants another person legal rights to make medical decisions on your behalf, or a financial POA, which grants someone the ability to make decisions related to finances. If you use one, which I highly recommend, make sure to have terms and conditions specifying your exact wishes. This prevents any miscommunication or someone acting in a way that is counter to what you want.

An attorney can help draft these important documents. If you cannot afford one, try looking for an online service that provides legal templates that you can modify. Companies such as LegalZoom, Nolo, and Rocket Lawyer have good reviews and are easily accessible and relatively inexpensive. I am not endorsing any product or service and have no experience with these companies; however, my point is you have options if an attorney is unavailable or too expensive. My best recommendation is to use an estate or family attorney to help you draft these documents.

Mindful Practice 28   Secure a will, power of attorney, and executor today.

DO YOU NEED A TRUST?

A trust is something else that you might want to consider developing in this step of wealth. *A trust* is an arrangement in which you authorize somebody to hold and distribute assets to the beneficiaries you choose upon your death. Your financial advisor can give you good advice on when you need a trust versus when you want to distribute assets through your will and beneficiary designations. Generally, if are concerned about covering monthly expenses of a beneficiary after your death, as an example, but might not want to leave all of your estate to a single person, you would use a trust. Trusts are useful for making monthly payments to a child with special needs or providing your spouse with lifetime income then reverting asset ownership to your children upon your spouse's death. You can design a trust for any type of arrangement. Whereas an executor of a will has an appointment for the period after the will until all assets are distributed, a trustee can provide services for decades or longer. Trusts are somewhat complicated and need to be setup by a professional after consulting with your advisor.

What is important is to prepare your plan for. Sure, some people have a chronic disease and might be able to predict their deaths a few months or years in advance. But for most of us, we have no idea when we are going to die. We must be prepared.

Monitoring Wealth

Just like a plant only grows and thrives when you give it water and light, your wealth can grow only when you tend to it. Monitoring wealth is important because it forces you to stick to a plan. Consistency, discipline, and self-control are required. If you don't have that yourself, you need to find an advisor or coach who does, or you should use a robo-investor. A *robo-investor* is the use of technology that uses your preferences to determine optimal investment allocations and recommendations. These tools are offered by any number of firms today, such as Goldman Sachs, Betterment, SoFi, and Charles Schwab.

There are a couple of ways to measure the lifetime effect of your financial decisions. Some of you might view this as the size of your checking or savings account. To others, it is your amount of annual salary. The best way to know the impact is to look at things more holistically based on your overall financial position. As we discussed earlier, the primary performance metric to evaluate your change in wealth is marketable net worth, or total marketable assets minus total liabilities—or what you own minus what you owe.

Good financial monitoring requires you to track this metric on an ongoing basis. I recommend using an automated software tool such as Quicken or Mint to help integrate your various accounts and then report your changes in financial position over time. If you don't use one of these, you could do it on paper or in a spreadsheet. The important information to document is your asset values, your debts, and your net worth. I recommend maintaining a beginning of month value, beginning of a quarter value, or beginning of year value based on your preferences. I use monthly for my own evaluations. Given the stock market fluctuations, it is important to try to use a consistent approach to timing—always the first or last day of the month, the 15th, or whatever you choose as long as it's consistent over time. This way you are accurately reflecting the valuations of all accounts. Figure 10.2 shows a sample of this graphically.

When monitoring your wealth, you will notice fluctuations—some months are much better than others as the stock market rises. It might lose value as well. This variability is common, and maintaining your focus and persistence is important. Don't withdraw your money when the market goes down a few

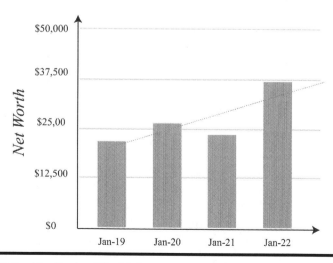

Figure 10.2 Monitoring Wealth Progress Over Time.

percentage points. As we showed earlier, the equity (stock) market has risen steadily during the past 30+ years; even when it goes down, it bounces back eventually!

When examining our wealth plans, we should factor this kind of uncertainty into our goals and plans. Routinely consider these kinds of questions:

- What if my salary goes down by 20% next year? How do I plan to pay my bills?
- What happens if the stock market goes into a recession? What would my plan be?
- If I have a medical emergency and need money fast, what would I do?

Using what I refer to as financial *scenario planning*, I always try to contemplate events that hopefully never happens, so that if they do, I will be more prepared. This technique involves making assumptions and estimates of potential future states at different points in the future to help prepare a contingency plan if the event comes true. When coaching clients, I always ask probing questions that deal with an uncertain future to help people prepare.

Mindful Practice 29   Be prepared for uncertainty with financial scenario planning.

Alternative Wealth Metrics

When you see improvements in your wealth, you might be develop a *confirmation bias*, in which you interpret information as proof of your existing beliefs. In essence, new data you receive are just confirmation that you were correct all along. Maybe the market went up, and even though you wanted to diversify into other areas, you kept all your money in aggressive growth technology funds, and they did well again. You might become biased in your thinking, that you are always right. This confirmation bias tends to impact us here in this stage of wealth, as does the over-confidence bias.

In addition to the three key numbers you should monitor (i.e., your overall equity, net spending percentage of money inflows, and net cash reserves monthly), you might consider examining other metrics. A common one is *debt-to-income ratio*, which is calculated by dividing your total monthly debt payments by your total equity (or income). Assume you had $2,000 in mortgage and another $500 in credit card debt monthly, and you earned $5,000 per month. It will produce a number, such as 50% debt to income. Calculate your current debt to income. If the number is anywhere above 40%, you need to find ways to reduce your debt.

You could also calculate a *debt-to-equity ratio*. This reflects the total liabilities divided by your total net worth, and hopefully will be less than 1. Any number greater than 1 indicates you have more debt than net worth. The lowest number possible is better—a range between 0.05 and 0.20 is common for wealthy individuals.

Now, these are both good ratios to consider, and they help you track your performance over time. But they both are a little flawed. Both measures record debt as the numerator, which is problematic because your focus in wealth management is to pay off all your debts. If you divide a zero (debt) by any number, you wouldn't be able to track your progress since it would result in a zero! Thus, they aren't always useful depending on where you are on your journey to wealth.

An alternative metric to measuring change in net worth over time is what I call the *equity-to-earnings* (E:E) *ratio*. This metric is useful for evaluating how successful you have been in converting your lifetime earnings into net worth; in effect, this is an efficiency measure. The E:E ratio compares your current net worth (or equity) against your lifetime earnings (or wages). This produces a ratio, which generally falls between 0 and 1. A negative value is possible, though, for those in an early career stage who have taken on debt, especially college loans or credit card debts. The higher the number, the better you have been at converting your earnings into net worth.

This E:E ratio is useful to evaluate where people are in terms of their overall financial health relative to their age. It also helps gauge behavior—your relative success in saving and investing. It normalizes your historical income against equity, which is why I find this metric particularly useful. To calculate E:E, start by adding up your liquid and marketable assets, plus your home and other assets, and subtract your liabilities. Follow these three steps:

1. Calculate equity (or net worth) by deducting your liabilities from assets. I prefer to use marketable assets (such as checking, savings, CDs, investments, retirements) and exclude assets that really can't be sold or are difficult to value.
2. Calculate your lifetime earnings. If you've paid into Social Security, an easy way to capture this is to log into the www.SSA.gov website, create an account, and download or add up your salary history (this provides the past 35 years of data). If you can't, simply estimate what you made each year from the time you started working. You can estimate it simply by taking estimates of your salary over time and multiplied by the number of years you've been working.
3. Divide #1 (equity) by #2 (total earnings).

Generally, most people in the early phase of their career have a ratio close to zero or even negative. When you first start working, you usually have little in savings and little in earnings. After a few years, people find themselves with credit card debt, automobiles, and even home mortgages. You might even have a negative net worth despite years of working. But, over time, people tend to save a little more and pay off some of the debt. A typical individual in their thirties might have a ratio of less than 5%–10%. As you age, if you are a stable earner and pay off debt as you can, your ratio might get to 25% by retirement years. Figure 10.3 is a generalized graph showing E:E ratios over time.

Although there is no "ideal" ratio, I compared some of the ultra-wealthy billionaires like Bill Gates or Jeff Bezos. Conservatively, if we say that the founder, chair, and former chief executive officer of Microsoft, for instance, made $2 million on average for the past 45 years he has been working (he is currently 65), it equates to $90 million in lifetime earnings. Of course, he made more in some years and less in the beginning when he was establishing the company and writing the software code that became one of the world's prominent brands, but this will work as an average. His net worth per *Forbes* magazine is conservatively estimated at $130 billion. Well, his ratio would be off the chart, with an equity of over 1400 times his lifetime earnings. Contrast that to the average American with a ratio at 65 more in line with 20%, and that gives you an idea of what we need to do to to create more wealth.

Yes, the obvious answer is to make more money. However, it also points to changing spending and investing behaviors. Great cash inflow is likely to lead to greater savings, but there is not a direct relationship. If there were, then many of the high-wage earners would retire comfortably rather than worrying about how

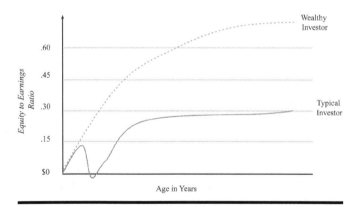

Figure 10.3 Equity to Lifetime Earnings.

to fund their same lifestyle when the paycheck dries up. Many of us make a lot of money, and still it does not improve our net worth. To manage wealth, we must continue to monitor these important financial health metrics.

Tax Strategy

Payroll, sales, income, franchise, capital gains, property, and other taxes can claim a large amount of your wealth. Most mindful choices we make should try to defer taxes to a later date or minimize them. Maximizing your pre-tax retirement contributions is one way we mentioned earlier to potentially deduct the investment and pay taxes later when you withdraw these funds, when your retirement tax bracket is much lower. You also need to explore increasing charitable donations (giving) and other deductions. At this stage, you should consider employing an accountant or financial advisor to help you review your approach to taxes and help you make the most of your money.

Liability Insurance

Insurance at a general level involves paying somebody else to take on your liability for personal, legal, property, or medical damages. Liability involves taking financial responsibility for loss. Insurance essentially transfers your future potential risk to a third party (i.e., an insurance company) by making payments today. Every month, we make payments for home, auto, life, health, and other forms of insurance, so in the event of a catastrophic event, we will not need to pay a much larger sum of money for repairs or other claims. Insurance utilizes the laws of probabilities and big numbers—and through large pools of insured individuals, prices can be kept reasonably low provided the frequency of accidents and claims pay-outs are also low.

No matter how much I dislike writing those checks each month, insurance is necessary. Why? Because if we don't have health insurance and we end up in the intensive care unit of a hospital for a month, that bill alone could cost us $1 million. Do you have $1 million available in your checking account? Even if you do, do you want to write that check? I don't. I'd rather make much more manageable, smaller payments monthly.

We need insurance across all 6 steps in the quest towards wealth. But, in this final step, we definitely need to maintain adequate levels of liability insurance. When you have high amount of net worth, you could become a target. Protect yourself by having the liability insurance you need. Check with your advisor or coach on this number. Many people, me included, recommend the use of umbrella liability insurance. *Umbrella insurance* provides an additional layer of protection beyond the limits necessary in all your other coverages. This coverage can help cover excess claims for property damage, personal liability, or lawsuits. This is essential and goes together with wealth management.

Mindful Practice 30   Consider your liability exposure with umbrella coverage.

Impact of Age on Financial Decisions

As discussed earlier and shown in Figure 2.3, while our capacity for risk and our wealth increases over time, we also tend to become a little more risk averse and conservative as we age. Maintaining your wealth over time, though, does not mean you must go into defensive strategy mode. You can and sometimes you will, but there are a number of people who remain offensive and assertive in all their moves regardless of wealth and age.

Although we tend to get wiser and more financially wealthy over time, we also tend to decline in other areas, including cognition (the process of thinking). Our emotions also change as we get older, and therefore age also plays a big role on our financial decisions. Nearly 1/5th of the population are considered "baby boomers" and are either in or approaching retirement. Since the majority of our wealth building and distribution occur in mid and older age, it is vital to understand the link between age and our ability to make good financial decisions. When we are young, we are less experienced but often quick to make decisions. We tend to be impulsive when we are young, and risks and consequences are less obvious or clear to us. Results from our choices are not always material or significant, as they tend to involve lower dollar amounts or short-term implications. As we age, investments are usually more significant, and risks and potential hazards cause us to think more about the downside consequences. We naturally become more conservative with regards to risk taking (i.e., more risk averse). This makes us contemplate decisions longer, although we have significantly more practice and learnings. One study found that older people benefit from more experience and less negative emotions when making financial decisions.[67] This is often contrasted though cognitive declines as people age.[68] Younger adults are more capable of more rapid, fluid cognition (faster decisions) but are generally less experienced, while older adults often rely on their experience and judgement but are somewhat slower cognitively. Some research suggests that middle age could offer the best of both worlds, having both experience and fluidity on their side.[69]

Age-related cognitive declines from Alzheimer's disease and dementia make financial decision-making extremely challenging.[70] For those with cognitive declines, judgment is impaired, and this could open up opportunities for making unnecessary purchases or being prone to fraud and scandals. Aversion and avoidance biases are common. We tend to hesitate and not act decisively. We are less sure about things. But more important, people tend to forget. Preparing lists, post-it notes, and reminders are even more essential for those of us in our later years. It is also imperative to have a financial coach or advisor who you trust, that has a POA to act on your behalf in the event of age-related declines that might impair your judgment. Planning for this involves implementing a structure that can support you (such as a family member who serves as an advocate or a trusted financial advisor) and should be part of everyone's estate planning process.

> *Be wary of spams and scams; phone calls and emails from people you don't know.*

We talked earlier about Medicare. Did you realize that Medicare does not cover long-term hospital care? Medicare will cover you up to a certain number of days, but if you need an extended (more than six months) stay or assisted living, you need to have sufficient financial resources or long-term care insurance. *Long-term care* insurance will cover your facility costs even if you have a cognitive chronic disease such as Alzheimer's disease. Medicare does not cover these costs, and they quickly add up. Without insurance coverage, stays can range from $5,000 to $15,000 per month, depending on the facility. Consider getting long-term care insurance any time after the age of 55 as a defensive strategy.

Decision Strategies

In step 6 of wealth, you are managing and monitoring changes in your financial health. Here are some other important strategies to consider.

1. **Wealth is elusive.** There is no magic number that will make you wealthy. I talk to people all the time who have $5 or $10 million in investments, and they still don't feel "wealthy." You will learn that the famous quote by Gertrude Stein, "There is no there, there" is correct.[71] If only we had $100,000 in net worth, we would feel wealthy. Then we get there, and feelings of wealth will escape us. If only we had $1 million or $5 million. Wealth is elusive. We also never know how much we need to maintain the

lifestyle we desire permanently. For this reason, many people tend to continue to accumulate based on their predispositions, backgrounds, tendencies, or even greed. Some researchers suggest that we must keep working and making more money to remain happy, which may be true. But since wealth has an emotional component, we all need to get better at knowing when enough is enough—when to stop accumulating, when to start giving, when to start sharing and just relax. We need to be reflective of where we came from and focus on our emotional health.

2. **Stop comparing yourself with others.** Wealth is relative. You might be wealthy, but there is always somebody wealthier. Growing up, my father used to repeat that in a slightly different way ("No matter how smart you think you are, there is always somebody smarter"). I learned early on to stop comparing myself with my classmates and my friends with regards to anything—athletics, intelligence, looks, and money. We need to do the same with wealth. We need to achieve "our" personal version of financial health—not anyone else's.

3. **Keep a long-term horizon**. A long-term horizon is important to weather the ups and downs of stock markets or changes in business cycles. Once you have selected your risk tolerance and asset allocation, avoiding selling off assets at wrong times or buying at unusually exuberant times. Both of these are harmful to maintaining wealth and keeping a long-term planning horizon. This is essential to wealth management.

4. **Factor in additional insurance.** You must examine your need for insurance of all forms, especially long-term care, medical, and additional liability insurance. We often neglect what life might look like without our employer-sponsored insurance plans, but we must overtly consider it at this stage. Think about supplemental insurance beyond Medicare and factor those costs into your allocations. Factor in long-term care insurance. It is also very important to consider additional liability at this stage. *Liability* is the risk of being at fault or responsible for something. When you have more wealth, people tend to be targeted more for lawsuits. Liability insurance in the forms of increased automobile coverages, medical liability, and even professional liability insurance needs to be considered. You might consider long-term care insurance as well. It is very important to consider what risks you want to retain or keep versus those you want to insure against. Generally, risks that would be extremely expensive and occur rarely should be insured. Consult your advisor or an insurance professional for an insurance needs analysis.

Table 10.1 summarizes the characteristics in step 6.

Table 10.1   Summary of Step 6

Summary	Get Wealthy
Overall financial Profile	Managing and monitoring wealth; focused on legacy and estate
Money mindset	More analytically driven; biased towards action
Decision style	Collaborative with multiple legal and financial advisors
Key strategies	Monitoring of important financial ratios; increasing liability insurance; protection against cognitive changes
Financial system	Use of trusts and estate plans
Current behavioral bias	Confirmation bias; overconfidence bias

Take Away

- Wealth continues to accumulate over time.
- Use financial ratios, such as debt-to-income and E:E ratios, to measure your changes routinely.
- Consider increasing the level of insurance and potentially include umbrella coverage to fully protect your assets.
- Develop all estate documents, including POA, a will, and other estate plans and name your beneficiaries on financial accounts.
- Giving (or being generous with your money) might become more important to some at this stage.
- Recognize when there is "enough" wealth and move towards a defensive financial strategy.
- Keep a long-term horizon and use ongoing decisions strategies to ensure that your brain doesn't derail the progress which you have made.

Key Terms

beneficiary, confirmation bias, Debt to equity ratio, debt-to-income ratio, equity-to-earnings (E:E) ratio, estate, estate plans, Executor, insurance, liability, long-term care, power of attorney, robo-investor, scenario planning, trust, umbrella insurance

Chapter 11

Decision-Making Strategies

"Saying 'yes' to one thing means saying 'no' to another. That's why decisions can be hard sometimes."

Sean Covey

All along this journey, we have been focusing on improving the system for financial decision-making while avoiding behavioral traps. In this chapter, we explore additional pragmatic decision strategies to keep you focused and financially healthy. Diversification, de-biasing, and overcoming past choices are the subjects of this chapter. We also discuss final heuristics and fallacies that can hinder our financial success.

Diversification

When saving and investing, strive to become diversified. *Diversification* is the strategy of incorporating greater variety into our choices. Variety helps to disperse or distribute our risk. Here's a simple example. Assume you had $300,000 in cash, and all of it was sitting in a single bank account. Then the bank completely collapsed. The federal insurance program (known as FDIC[1]) would only

---

[1] FDIC, Federal Deposit Insurance Corporation. It covers up to $250,000 per account per owner and is insured by the federal government.

cover a portion of this. If you diversified and spread your money into two separate accounts or institutions, you could be completely covered.

You should diversify, if possible, your sources of income as well. This is where a side hustle or part-time hobby that brings in money could be useful. In the event of something tragic at your main position (like a layoff or reduction in force), you would still have potential revenue.

The same concept goes for investing. You should not have all your money in the real estate market, no matter how good you think the local housing market is. You shouldn't have all your money in gold, even if you worry about the future of currency. You shouldn't have all your money in cryptocurrency or fixed income securities or keep all your cash in the freezer. Diversify. A diversified *portfolio* (or an assortment of stocks, mutual funds, or other investments) helps you to avoid significant losses because it spreads the risk, and you don't have "all of your eggs in one basket." With diversification, one asset might be increasing, which could offset a decreasing one. This reduces your risk exposure and limits the variability in overall losses.

When looking at stocks, be sure to balance different beta values—don't have all your investments with a beta (systematic risk) greater than the market as a whole ($B = 1$). For mutual funds, be sure to look at expense ratios (lower is better), overall historical returns, the risks (beta), and turnover rates. Turnover helps to examine how often the portfolio manager trades stocks—the higher the turnover, the more in capital gains taxes you will pay.

You can do your research necessary for diversifying on any of the reliable platforms, such as Morningstar, Yahoo Finance, or Market Watch. Alternatively, all the largest investment firms maintain their own research sites, which you should closely examine when making investments.

Train Your Bias

Bias, as we have shown throughout all the previous chapters, exists because our mind is not operating in a vacuum. We have emotional, genetic, environmental, and other factors that influence our choices. Depending on your unique brain and step of wealth, you might be prone to one or more of the behavioral biases. If you know bias exists, you should strive to remove it, particularly if you find that the quality of the choices or your financial outcomes are not where you want them to be.

One technique is known as a *counter bias*—gently directing our attention towards the action in order to avoid doing it.[72] Counter bias has also become known as a nudge.[73] If you notice you are eating more donuts, for example, a nudge might be to remind you that almonds are a better option. The other technique is called *de-biasing*, which centers on removing the influence of bias altogether. A simple example is that if you tend to make decisions based on who else might have invested in something, you will remove that factor from the data you reviewed when making the decision. Research has shown that simple training exercises can help you de-bias.[74] This way, you aren't exposed to that particular bias.

Here are some steps for trying to overcome your biases:

1. **Mindful awareness.** I know this is tough. We are good at focusing on other people's problems and behaviors, but have you stopped to look at your own? Practice reflection daily and see if you can notice a trend or pattern in how you respond. Try to become more mindful about your thoughts and words. Are they automatic (reflexive, impulsive) or more measured? Do you tend to do or say something specific? Be mindful about the biases, whether they are over-confidence or procrastination. Look at each of the biases we discussed in this book and see which one most applies to you.

2. **Ask others.** Do you sometimes get questions, glares, or stares from others when you respond a certain way? Has your advisor or coach asked you to re-think a certain choice? Has your spouse or partner commented on your confidence, self-control, risk persuasion, or anything else? You might try asking for feedback from others if they observe any of the behavioral biases mentioned regarding your actions or choices. Ask for input from others around you.

3. **Congruence.** Are you consciously stopping before a choice to consider both emotions and reasoning every time? Try to write down your thoughts and reasoning behind the money choices you are making. Check them daily to see if you are making more analytical or more emotional choices. We need to try to balance and achieve congruence to make mindful money management choices.

4. **Daily reminders.** All of us get very busy from one day to the next. We often forget to do even the most common things, such as picking up a specific item from the store or brushing our teeth. So, it's not a surprise that we forget to be mindful when making a choice. Use an app or pen and paper and write daily remembers. I frequently jot down notes to remind myself to be more thoughtful, to breathe deeply for 30 seconds, or to step away from the computer. Similarly, use financial reminders to balance your checking account, do your research before a big purchase, or weekly look at your investment accounts.

Reduce the Impact of Decision Fatigue

When we are physically, mentally, or emotionally fatigued we make poor decisions. This has been studied in a variety of different environments, as well as in finance.[75] Basically, when we are exhausted in any form, we are more prone to accept bad deals, make rash judgments, compromise our normal standards, or accept unreasonable offers in negotiations. We also get *decision fatigue*, in which we are just tired of making decisions altogether, and the quality of our choices can become compromised.

If you fly into Heathrow Airport in London after being on a plane for 12 hours, you are exhausted. If a rental agency offers a rental car, you are more likely to accept a higher price than you might if you were refreshed and relaxed. If you hadn't yet booked a hotel, you might walk into one and pay the "rack rates" (the highest standard rate) rather than the discount rates you get when you search in advance. We are just not on the top of our game when we are fatigued. The best way to avoid the impact of fatigue on decisions is to plan ahead. Make arrangements in advance and stay fresh. Watch out for people and firms that try to take advantage of your fatigue.

Forget About Past Losses

One of the biggest issues we have is that we tend to dwell on our past mistakes and losses. We have all lost something in our lives. We might have invested in a mutual fund and lost 10% of our equity. We might have bought a car that we regret that turned out to be a lemon. Or we might have gone to Vegas and gambled $1,000 on the roulette table and lost it all. The outcome of our decision might have included getting less than we had hoped or expected.

When this stops us from making any future choices, this becomes a bias. Loss aversion, procrastination, and avoidance biases all relate to missing out on potential gains just to avoid a possible loss. This is an avoidance behavior, based on risk aversion, which ultimately could cost people future returns. As we become wealthy, we think long term and recognize that gains and losses balance out and that over time if we make wise choices, we will prevail.

Don't let past losses dissuade you from future choices. Do your research. Identify alternatives. The past loss is gone, and it shouldn't bias your future choices.

CASE IN POINT

A 57-year-old woman named Ellen made her first stock investment, in a small public airline company based on a tip from another family member. It went bankrupt within two years of the initial investment, and she lost all $5,000 that she put in. The stock turned into what is called a "penny stock" and then stopped trading altogether. There was no recourse. As a common stockholder, she didn't have any claims on the airline assets. Ellen never invested again. This avoidance mindset resulted in a permanent loss aversion bias.

Overcome Cognitive Dissonance

All of us can probably recall specific poor choices that we have made somewhere along the line, whether that's getting into a car with an impaired driver, staying out too late, or buying something we didn't need or could afford. We tend to put a lot of emotional weight behind really good and really bad decisions. We overweight the influence we had on those good decisions but sometimes de-emphasize our roles in the poor choices. This is called the *positivity effect*, and it really does influence the way we make choices going forward. We remember the good feelings and emotions far longer than we do the bad ones, which makes it difficult to prevent making the same kind of mistakes repeatedly! Therefore, some of us repeat the same patterns of poor choices over and over or try to avoid making a decision at all in many cases.

Sometimes we purchase something, and we (nearly) immediately regret it or wish that we would have done something different. *Cognitive dissonance* is the tension or stress we feel when we did something that might conflict with other parts of our brains or even new information we received right after the purchase or investment. For example, if Mary K. puts $5,000 into an airline stock and the next day sees a news story about how travel might be going down, she might instantly feel the tension between what she did and what she now perceives as more accurate information. Or, more commonly, we want to save money in one part of our brains; another region wants to go out and spend it all. No matter what we do, the tension or dissonance will still be there. We all get cognitive dissonance to some degree. The best way to avoid regret, though, is to consciously think through the choice and fully contemplate the consequences before we make the decision—not afterwards.

A mindful approach to each choice will ensure that you have exhausted all options and are fully conscious and aware of the choice you are about to make. Once you have that feeling of being fully mindful, then you must move to the stage of acceptance of our choice.

Cognitive dissonance is really a fear—a thought or belief based in fear that you made the wrong choice. Fear and uncertainty are major obstacles to building wealth. I find these to be a particularly negative and useless set of thoughts. It's easier to say that than to internalize it, especially after you made a decision you might regret. But to truly be happy, we must figure out how to reduce the amount of our time spent in dissonance.

Reverse and Overcome Past Mistakes

We all make bad choices sometimes. We chose one path over another, and ultimately, we were not satisfied with the outcome. It happens. We might have overpaid for something and later find it 50% off somewhere else. We might have purchased a lower quality item than we hoped. There are many examples I am sure you can come up with when you made a wrong decision. Sometimes, as we just mentioned, we should just forget about the choice and move on.

Other times no matter what we do, we cannot go back in time and reverse a bad decision. Although we all wish that we could jump in a tesseract or time capsule and travel through space and time, we simply can't. So, if we know this to be true, and we understand that dissonance (regret or tension) is not particularly helpful, why do we focus so much on it? Why do we tend to regret bad decisions much longer than we reward good ones? The answer is rooted in our brain, of course.

We tend to over-estimate the amount of impact that we had on any one good outcome. If something goes well, we like to take the credit. If something goes poorly, if possible, we tend to blame someone else. This *self-serving bias* is when we take credit for good choices but blame others for the poor ones. This is something that plays out a lot in organizational decision-making. But what if we have no one to blame but ourselves? We tend to dwell on our past mistakes. Ruminating on bad choices brings these thoughts into consciousness, which highlights the negative effect even more. It's a vicious cycle.

What can you do? Here are some pragmatic tips to avoid regrets.

1. **Ask for your money back.** You would be surprised how many times you *can* reverse a bad choice. Ask if it is possible to get a refund—or even a partial refund. Did you know that just by "asking" the question, you are significantly more likely than not to get a refund, discount, or money back? Most people never even ask, which ensures you will never get your money returned. If it's an expense and not an investment per se, you can often request your money back contractually. Even a large purchase such as a car or a house might have a special provision that allow you to reconsider things for a short period of time. Check your receipts or contracts to see what they say. But don't stop there—go back and specifically ask. Phone calls do not work as well as in person. When we are face to face with somebody, they are much more likely to say "yes" than "no." Make sure

you've exhausted all these efforts. Many times, you can make a compelling case and get your full money returned.

2. **Practice mindfulness.** Throughout this book, we are learning to cultivate a mindful practice of money management. This means to become aware of what we're doing right with our practices and wrong with our negative habits. It also means becoming aware of discipline, persistence, and emotions before, during, and after all money decisions. Mindfulness is not necessarily meditation, but they are similar; the practice of sitting with your decisions, allowing yourself to fully appreciate what has just transpired, and then accepting that fate is essential to moving on. Once you have accepted that something is in fact gone, finished, or lost, it will play a smaller and less important role in your mind over time. Stop ruminating constantly by focusing one final time on this choice. Stop replaying the mistake in your brain once this exercise has been done.

3. **Journal.** Document in your financial decision journal. As with all choices related to money, detail the choice, your moods, and emotions, what you felt went right and what went wrong. Think about what lessons you learned from it and then move on!

4. **Maintain perspective.** As a final step, put this into perspective. Last, put the decision into perspective. About 99.9% of all our choices are not catastrophic. Only a few ever are. Put this into perspective by really processing the impact. Will this break you? Will this choice have forced you into an irreversible landslide? It is doubtful. It will probably cost you some money, some lost time, and some sleep, but the bad choice will not break you. Keep this in your mind and repeat positive mantras like this daily:

"I will survive. I will move forward. I will succeed."

Maximize Your Options

If you could spend your time on any one part of the decision-making system, it should be to seek out all alternatives for each choice. A greater variety of other options opens your mind to different possibilities, and it also provides leverage for better negotiation on price. Greater choice results in more opportunities— and the more, the better with financial decisions.

When we make an insurance decision, get multiple quotes from different companies. When purchasing airline tickets, shop around. When investing, compare the investments through one of the multiple ratings agencies (listed in Appendix B) to see what has the best mix of risk and return to match your style.

Of course, the flip side is that more alternatives can become overwhelming to some, creating anxiety or uncertainty. The term *analysis paralysis* was coined in fact because of some people's tendency to churn over information repeatedly and avoid making decisions altogether, searching for more and better data.[76] I am not suggesting that you go that far. In fact, I prepare myself mentally that I will never have 100% of the information I need to make a good choice, and that is okay! We just enough alternatives to get points of comparison. I do suggest you always have at least one or two additional alternatives to improve the decision quality. Spend as much time as needed to identify options before making your choice.

Get an Outsider's Perspective

When we pull back from a situation and have a little space, we sometimes see things differently. When we're in the heat of an argument, for example, we sometimes don't see the other person's perspectives. But with time and distance, we gain a new appreciation and perspective. The same is true for financial decisions. There are times we need an outside and independent viewpoint. Collaborating with an advisor, coach, accountant, or planner can help to review your goals, tactics, and overall financial plan. They can also help you with recommendations and advice for specific services, such as insurance or legal expertise.

Financial advisors are not scary, and most of the good ones work on a fee-only basis. You pay a fee for a set of recommendations, and you can either choose to go with it or do something else. More people need to get second opinions on their financial health.

Consider Both Demand and Supply

I hear a lot of people tell me that they don't need a plan; they "just need more money." Only if they had more money (i.e., supply), all their financial problems would go away! There is a common perception that more money is the solution, when in fact, more money will only magnify your problems. If you don't tackle the behavioral and the spending side (i.e., demand), you will repeat the same pattern only with larger dollar amounts when you make more money. Spending more than you budgeted routinely tends to be a behavioral problem, which needs to be tackled inside your own head. Being mindful of choices will help. And, yes, having money coming in does help, but the real work lies in addressing our patterns and habits of choices. Many of our problems are with too much going out. Focus on both sides of the equation. Consider the impact of both supply and demand, or "money in" and "money out." You can become wealthy even if your salary over the years never crosses into six figures.

Simulation Models

I described the use of mindful allocation models earlier and my general guideline of 60-15-15-10 (60% spending, 15% investing, 15% retirement, and 10% giving). In this technique, you examine historical money patterns and determine a mix to maximize wealth based on your goals. For example, if you have a short-term need for college tuition for a child, you'd increase the investing portion and reduce the other areas accordingly. I also suggest using financial scenario planning to identify several key assumptions (e.g., an estimate of risks and uncertainty, the time horizon, dollar values) and predict changes in wealth. A *simulation model* is a mathematical technique used on a computer that can predict performance given certain assumptions. Most models incorporate Monte Carlo modeling, which has a calculation engine performing probability distributions and sampling techniques. You could also use a spreadsheet with formulas to include minimization and maximization techniques.

Many financial advisors have simple models that can help us predict retirement needs using a few assumptions, but relatively few advisors have models for optimizing all four money areas. Seek out collaboration from a well-qualified behavioral financial advisor who can help you in this area.

Avoid Procrastination and Don't Delay

There are people who pay bills and take care of financial transactions as they arrive and then those who procrastinate. There is a relationship between people who have financial trouble and the avoidance mindset. There may be times when you can't avoid procrastinating. It's natural to avoid unpleasant, complex, or challenging tasks. Avoidance theories tell us that people tend to delay doing things which are troublesome, which in turn can have physiological effects, such as sweating or an increased heart rate.[77]

Procrastination bias is rooted in the belief that our brains look for immediate gratification—or positive rewards—from tasks and when they receive rewards, we will do more of those over time. We essentially are valuing short-term gains more than those in the long term. Our brains are wired for networks and neuroscientists often say that nerve cells which "fire together, wire together." That implies that things we routinely perform simultaneously will create common associations and become more routine. The longer you avoid something, the harder it will ever be to change the network. There is truth to the adage that it takes 21 days to form a habit. We need time to start any new activity to let it become part of our neural network, become routine, and develop a good habit. Whether it's meditation or tracking your finances, you need to overcome the procrastination bias today.

Avoid the Monopoly Effect

In personal finance, we make choices daily. Sometimes the choice might be as simple as choosing to do nothing or to not act, not spend money, or not go out to eat. What is clear, though, is that we are biased by small numbers. When we have small bills (like $1 or $5) in our wallet, we tend to value those less than larger ones and are more likely to spend more. If we have five $10 bills, for example, we will likely spend that faster than we would with the $50 bill. We tend to hold on to larger denominations longer. Researchers have found that consumers are more likely to buy things in smaller dollar increments without even considering the ramifications. In contrast, a purchase of a home or an RV would at least require more thought.[78]

I suggest thinking in big denominations. Think about your paycheck as one single bill rather than several thousand $1 bills, which are easy to spend. We are more likely to spend more if we cash our paycheck, especially if we get small bills. The denomination effect makes it easier to spend smaller amounts than large ones. Therefore, earlier I recommended direct depositing your paycheck and electronically withdrawing and investing regular amounts monthly as opposed to cashing the check and holding on to currency. By using only electronic funds, this, too, can potentially create a behavioral problem. Credit cards and mobile apps (e.g., Google Pay, Apple Pay) have made lives a lot more automated. We don't need to head into the bank to get cash to purchase our groceries or clothing. We don't need a large wallet to carry our money. Payments are typically faster with credit versus exchanging correct currency at a cash register. We have greatly improved the ease and simplicity of making streamlined purchases due to credit. The downside is that it also allows us to purchase things that we otherwise could not afford. We are extended credit in many cases far beyond our means. The consequence is that they tend to make us over-spend.

Research has shown that it is much easier to spend money when using credit than actual cash. I call this the *monopoly effect*—when you use a currency that can seem like "play" money. Neuroscientists have shown through magnetic resonance imaging (MRI) that parts of our fore brains' central region for cognition are activated more by credit card purchases than by cash.[79] This is problematic because if our motivations to spend increase with credit and we are not highly disciplined, our brain may motivate us to spend even when it's unnecessary or unwise.

Virtual currencies, such as cryptocurrency and credit cards, could entirely replace cash transactions, creating a monopoly effect. It is likely that one of the reasons most people spend more than they make is due to this effect.

Decision Strategies—A Final Checklist

Since each decision we make is cumulative over a lifetime and they all add up to the sum of where we are going, we must become more reflective when we make both big and small purchases and investments. Your approach, the final moments leading up to a money choice, can make all the difference in terms of outcomes.

Last, your wealth is determined by how you confront each opportunity. Next outline 12 important steps that you can use a checklist each day and before every financial decision you make. Annually, create a vision. Monthly, re-visit your plans and numbers. Daily, set an intention. Wake up and say, "Today I will take care of my business. I will [take the action] which I keep putting off!" Setting an intention to be mindful of our choices is one thing. Acting on them and executing good financial strategies is another.

1. Slow down and try to contemplate the choice, whether it's over a few dollars or a few thousand dollars. All choices, big and small, move us in the right direction. Ask yourself: is this the right time for me to be making this decision? Is it really the right one, or is something clouding my judgment?
2. Put your reminders in front of you that you have written down on note cards or your phone. Remind yourself of everything important—questions to ask the salesperson, feature to investigate, risks or details about an investment—anything you might not remember.
3. Practice some deep breathing exercises while you are contemplating a choice. Try to remove any false expectations, such as the need for an instantaneous decisions.
4. Spend some time outdoors or doing something to reverse your polarity to ensure wise choices. Try to contemplate your goals, your alternatives, and the impact a choice will have on your wealth.
5. Create a short list detailing the decision you are trying to make. Writing things down helps you to clarify your thought process.
6. Make a list of the choices that you have available to you. Consider using a decision tree.

7. Determine the value of the opportunity cost. What are you missing out on by making this decision? What else could you be doing with this money? How would this impact your wealth?

8. Talk the list out with your partner, spouse, friend, child, or financial advisor. Get their opinions on your rationale for buying or spending money and on the choices you think you must make. Often others might have a different viewpoint that could come up with better choices or even identify reasons not to make the decision you thought you were going to make.

9. Make sure you have the end result in mind. Make sure the list has your desired outcome on it. Always consider the impact on your net worth and other key metrics we discussed when making any choice. Ask yourself, "Does this choice increase my wealth?"

10. Double check to make sure that once you've narrowed down the choice to one, you go back and make sure it addresses your goal. Answer these questions: will leasing this new office space really help me grow my business? Is the purchase of this car over another car helping me improve or worsen my financial position? The use of a decision checklist to document and codify your thought process can be helpful.

11. Take action—small steps today to get momentum. Don't keep putting off that "thing" you have meant to do.

12. Track your progress over time. Write things down or record them in a spreadsheet or mobile phone app. Monitor changes over time to see how you're progressing.

Take Away

- Diversifying your sources of income, expenditures, and investments will improve portfolio returns and stabilize risks.

- Physical and mental fatigue can create poor choices. Plan ahead and give yourself space when making choices.

- Decision fatigue can be lessened by limiting distractions, being rested and relaxed, and preparing in advance.

- Forgetting your past mistakes and losses will help you embrace an offensive financial strategy that attracts wealth.

- Always directly consider the opportunity cost (i.e., what you could have done with that money) before making a choice.

- De-biasing techniques can help to identify errors in judgment that you might routinely make unconsciously. Use de-biasing steps to reverse and eliminate the negative impact that biases play in finance.

- Consider using a financial journal, decision checklist, reminders, and mantras daily to make more mindful money choices.

Key Terms

analysis paralysis, cognitive dissonance, counter-bias, de-bias, decision fatigue, denomination effect, diversification, loss aversion, monopoly effect, portfolio, positivity effect, self-serving bias, simulation model

Chapter 12

Mindful Money Practices

"If you obey all the rules, you miss all the fun."

Katharine Hepburn

You Made It

Congratulations. You have made it. You are wealthy or on the path to wealth. Nobody is standing in the way of your wealth. Remember that wealth is an attitude—it becomes your identity. To become a wealthy person, you must think like one. You must adopt the discipline, persistence, and healthy habits. In the preceding 12 chapters, we outlined the 6 steps, 2 major bridges, and 30 mindful money practices. We also must avoid 20 critical behavioral traps and 10 high-risk negative habits during the quest. You did this! You can shift your brain to manage your money mindfully.

Throughout this book, we have walked through many financial practices, which can help lead you towards mindful choices and wealth. I call these mindful money practices, and these guidelines offer you one proven path to wealth. While it would be virtually impossible always to follow these practices for each decision, the good news is that you need to apply *most* of these *most* of the time. Consistency is important.

We have climbed 6 steps or stage on the quest, taking you from getting by to getting wealthy. At first, we dealt with frustration, acceptance, commitment,

DOI: 10.4324/9781003231844-15

and execution. We then cultivated the right money mindset, a real obstacle for most people. Then we articulated financial goals and went through mindful money allocation to maximize daily choices. You are moving to a higher level when following the financial pyramid. Remember to properly sequence your financial strategies to avoid timing issues that will improve your momentum. Making wise daily choices is essential. You can't make one big right decision that will reverse your financial problems—but a series of small choices adds up over time. A financial advisor might be necessary to help you on the journey.

Wealth is achievable, and mindful money choices can get you there through consistency and perseverance. Take a moment to review the critical points in the Mindful Money Management Model™ shown in Figure 12.1.

Throughout this book, we have covered 30 mindful money practices. Try to adopt all of these practices and strategies to ensure you become wealthy.

MP1. Find your "why" for wealth before starting the quest.

MP2. Look for patterns and problems in your current process of choosing.

MP3. For each choice, ask yourself: will this improve my future wealth?

MP4. Take one small step at a time.

MP5. Remember that wealth is the sum of all big and small decisions

MP6. Prepare for the "approach." Pause, breathe, and contemplate before choosing.

MP7. Recognize that others can be behavioral counterforces to mindful money management.

MP8. Cultivate a multi-sensory mindset.

MP9. Activate both your emotional and analytical hemispheres before making a choice.

MP10. Incorporate a daily financial decision journal.

MP11. Do not wait for complete certainty before making a choice.

MP12. Confront your financial fears.

MP13. Never sell assets during a down market!

MP14. Remember this: 99.9% of the time, a bad decision will not destroy you.

MP15. Consciously resist the temptation to procrastinate.

MP16. Verbally and mentally commit to changes.

MP17. Choose financial curiosity. Read, watch, and learn about finance daily.

MP18. Practice daily intentions.

MP19. Mindful change = Self-awareness + Motivation + Action

MP20. Re-imagine your financial identity and beliefs.

MP21. Document, rank, and attack your negative habits.

MP22. Expose, don't bury, past financial mistakes.

MP23. Write down specific goals and hold yourself accountable.

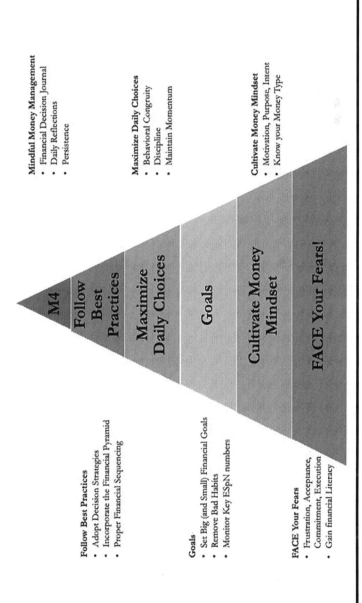

Figure 12.1 The Mindful Money Management Model™.

Mindful Money Management
• Financial Decision Journal
• Daily Reflections
• Persistence

Maximize Daily Choices
• Behavioral Congruity
• Discipline
• Maintain Momentum

Cultivate Money Mindset
• Motivation, Purpose, Intent
• Know your Money Type

M4

Follow Best Practices

Maximize Daily Choices

Goals

Cultivate Money Mindset

FACE Your Fears!

Follow Best Practices
• Adopt Decision Strategies
• Incorporate the Financial Pyramid
• Proper Financial Sequencing

Goals
• Set Big (and Small) Financial Goals
• Remove Bad Habits
• Monitor Key ESpN numbers

FACE Your Fears
• Frustration, Acceptance, Commitment, Execution
• Gain financial Literacy

MP24. Dream big. Then take small steps each day!

MP25. Always maintain assets > liabilities.

MP26. Maximize financial momentum through propulsion, gravity, direction, and time.

MP27. Don't churn or withdraw invested money.

MP28. Secure a will, power of attorney, and executor today.

MP29. Be prepared for uncertainty with financial scenario planning.

MP30. Consider your liability exposure with umbrella coverage.

Thank you for reading!

Appendix A: Glossary of Key Terms

Affirmation: A statement that you repeat to yourself daily to provide yourself emotional support and motivation.

Afford: Commonly defined as the ability to pay for something. Alternatively, should be viewed as whether a choice results in an improved position of wealth.

Alternatives: Multiple options or possibilities. Two or more potential courses of actions.

Alpha: Excess level of returns given the relative risks and market returns.

Ambiguity effect: Our tendency to subconsciously avoid unclear paths.

Analysis paralysis: A term used when people churn over information repeatedly and avoid making decisions altogether, searching for more and better data.

Analytical: The process of analyzing alternatives in terms of risks, opportunity costs, and benefits when making a choice.

Anchoring bias: Our fixation on specific information we first learn about, which frames our perceptions and choices.

Assumption: A numerical estimate for what we believe will happen in the future.

Automation bias: Tendency to rely on electronic systems as our primary means of truth, when in fact we might make a completely different and better decision had we manually intervened.

Autopilot: Choices made without thought or deliberation.

Availability bias: The tendency to make a choice based on our narrow perspective of what is known and available to us at the time of choice.

Avoidance: Mindset that causes us to neglect our finances.

Balance sheet: A financial statement that details all assets, liabilities, and resulting net worth.

Bankruptcy: Legal action in which a court determines that somebody is unable to pay for outstanding debt and determines an appropriate course of action.

Behavior: How we act, given what is going on in our brain and the surrounding environment.

Behavioral bias: A mental trap or illogical response often made unconsciously, which limits a more thoughtful choice. A belief, feeling, or thought that interferes with our more rational decision-making process.

Behavioral counterforce: People, our thinking, or anything else that stands in our way of sound decision systems

Behavioral economics: Reflect the study of our behaviors when making choices involving resources.

Behavioral finance: The impact of psychology and context in choices involving money.

Benchmarking: Evaluating other's performance and actions in an effort to improve our own.

Beneficiary: The person who receives the rights to that asset after you die.

Bequest: Gift or inheritance left to a beneficiary.

Beta: Degree of systematic risk for the investment relative to the overall market.

Bond: A loan (or debt instrument) that a company uses to borrow money from consumers.

Bounded rationality: Limits of rational decision-making, either due to lack of computational capabilities or failure to fully understand the entire problem.

Budget: Written estimate of your planned expenses and revenue over a specific time period.

Certainty: Condition in which you are always correct, with no doubts.

Cognition: The mental process where we collect, analyze, and act on our thoughts and emotions.

Cognitive dissonance: Tension or stress we feel when we did something that might conflict with other parts of our brains. Regret over a purchase or investment.

Commitment: Being obligated or emotionally impelled to do something.

Compounding: The process of growth in financial assets related to time and cumulative rates of return.

Consciousness: The state of understanding and realizing something.

Consumer disclosure: A statement from a financial organization (especially those that loan money) which provides the rates and fees of the service.

Counter bias: An action taken to direct attention towards the action in order to avoid doing it.

De-bias: An action taken to remove the influence of a bias altogether.

Debt-to-equity ratio: A financial ratio that divides your overall liabilities by net equity. Lower numbers are better.

Debt-to-income ratio: A financial ratio that compares monthly debt payments to monthly income. Lower numbers are better.

Decision: A choice between two or more alternatives.

Decision approach: How you prepare for an interaction involving any money choice.

Decision fatigue: The exhaustion felt from making too many, or too complex, choices.

Decision-making: The process of selecting goals, identifying alternatives, and making choices.

Decision quality: Reflects the process or system we used to make the choice. Incorporates our decision approach, financial organization, and judgment.

Decision tree: Visual flowchart resembling a tree, which presents the options in front of you and the probability (or likelihood) that a particular outcome or event will result.

Default effect: The tendency to choose what we are most familiar with. To gravitate towards the default.

Deterministic: Choices that have complete certainty in outcomes.

Debt: Financial obligations owed to someone else. Also known as a liability.

Debt avalanche: A strategy to pay debts off first that have the highest interest rate.

Debt snowball: A strategy to pay off debts first with the lowest principal balances.

Defensive: A type of financial strategy that tends to protect and shore up your financial position rather than to increase it.

Defined benefit: A type of retirement plan that pays a specified monthly amount based on a formula comprised of tenure, average salary, and other factors.

Defined contribution: A type of retirement plan where employer contributes into a plan, and the employee is responsible for investment risks and returns.

Diversification: Strategy of incorporating greater variety into our choices.

Dividend: Earnings that a company distributes out to the owners or shareholders of a firm, which effectively reduces their net income.

Dollar-cost averaging: The practice of routine periodic investing on a routine basis, no matter if the market goes up or down.

Elimination: A strategy for complete removal or avoidance of a negative habit in its entirety.

Emergency reserve: Money set aside in a specific savings or money market account that accumulates through routine deposits. A contingency fund in the event of an unforeseen large expense.

Emotion: Psychological state often based on feelings rather than active thought.

Equity: One meaning refers to capital raised through stock ownership in a firm. The other is synonymous with net worth (assets minus liabilities).

Equity-to-earnings (E:E) ratio: A financial ratio useful for evaluating how successful (efficient) you have been in converting all of your lifetime earnings into net worth. Compares your current net worth (or equity) against your lifetime earnings (or wages).

ESpN: Equity, spending, and net cash flow. Key numbers needed to measure and monitor wealth.

Estate: Total of all of your equity in your accumulated assets. Represents what you own.

Estate plans: Documents used to manage the ongoing protection and eventual distribution of your net worth at some point in the future.

Exchange-traded funds: A type of mutual fund that is passively managed, has lower operating expense ratios than most index funds, and is traded actively on an exchange.

Executor: Person (or institution) you name to manage the distribution of your assets after your death in your will.

FACE: Frustration, acceptance, commitment, and execution. Keys to overcoming barriers to motivation and get started on quest for wealth.

Fallacy: A financial untruth, often due to over-use of heuristics.

Fear: Emotion that causes us to run from danger and to avoid risks.

Fee only: An arrangement with a financial advisor that is based solely on fees and not on sales commission or other financial arrangements.

Financial discipline: Mindful adherence to your intended allocation plans for spending, savings, investing, and giving of your financial resources

Financial inertia: The persistence of stability and inaction. Associated with procrastination and avoidance behaviors.

Financial literacy: Knowledge required to make informed judgments and to take effective decisions regarding the use and management of money.

Financial planning: Systematic roadmap for future financial decision-making. Comprehensive process of analyzing goals and developing strategies to meet those goals.

Financial pyramid: Figure that presents an optimal sequence (under general circumstances) of when to make some of the most common money management decisions we face.

Financial strategy: Pattern of financial decisions made over time.

Get-rich-quick: A scheme where somebody tries to make an unusual amount of money in a short period of time rather than through hard work, discipline, and good financial decisions.

Goals: Desired results or specific intentions you hope to achieve.

Habit: A routine or tendency which we perform on a repeated basis without conscious thought.

Heuristic: Mental shortcut designed to help us understand something complex. Financial guideline or rule of thumb.

HNWI: High net worth individual. Typically refers to somebody with $1 million in net worth.

Illusion of control: A behavioral bias in which we think we are more in control of outcomes than we really are.

Index fund: A mutual fund that buys a large, diversified portfolio of stocks in an effort to match the performance of a stock index, such as the Dow Jones or Standard and Poor's. Index funds have two key advantages: they reduce risks of owning specific stocks, and they are less expensive with low trading fees.

Individual retirement account: An investment account expressly set aside for retirement that grows either tax-deferred or tax-free, depending on whether it is traditional or Roth. Must meet specific Internal Revenue Service guidelines.

Insurance: The practice of transferring risk to a third-party to cover legal, medical, property, and other liabilities.

Intention: Commitment or a desired statement of beliefs and aspirations that provide direction. Verbal statements that help to create a commitment to action.

Interest: Amount of money received by you to keep your money at a financial institution or paid to an institution (in the case of a loan).

Judgment: Interpretation of circumstances, given our past experiences, personalities, and reasoning.

Leverage: Use of debt to maximize purchasing power.

Liability: The risk of being at fault or responsible for something. In this context used for liability insurance planning.

Load: An upfront charge for purchasing a mutual fund, similar to a commission.

Longevity risk: The risk that we will outlive our available savings.

Long-term care: A form of insurance that provides coverage of long-term hospitalization expenses associated with disabilities, chronic diseases, and Alzheimer's disease.

Loss aversion: The preference to avoid all losses, even at the expense of larger potential gains.

Match: Represents the percent that your company will put into a plan, as a percentage of what you contribute.

Mindful: Deliberate actions made with full awareness. Being fully present and aware of our choices.

Mindfulness: The deliberate act of being fully present and aware of what we are doing.

Mindful Money Management Model™ (M4): The path, best practices, habits, and personal decision strategies used on the quest for wealth.

Mobilizing: The process of gathering and assembling all important financial information about what you spend, what you own, who and how much you owe.

Moderation: A strategy for reducing or removing some of the excess and extreme impact of the negative financial habit.

Momentum: Progression of wealth, composed of propulsion, gravity, direction, and time.

Monetize: Determine the financial impact.

Money management: The process of planning and controlling financial resources, centering on where, when, and how we save, invest, give, and spend our money.

Money mindset: The spiritual connotation relating to our beliefs, values, goals, and aspirations. Our set of attitudes, philosophy, and approach to money choices.

Monopoly effect: A bias for over-spending when using a currency that can seem like "play" money.

Motivation: The energy or drive that sustains individuals as we pursue changes in behaviors and pursuit of goals. Why we do what we do.

Mutual fund: Portfolio of different stocks or bonds that are typically professionally managed by a financial expert and offered by an investment firm or broker.

Negativity bias: Our tendency to focus on negative rather than positive thoughts and memories.

Neural networks: Connections between cells which help our brain learn, store memories, and decide.

Net worth: The difference between what you own and what you owe. Also called equity, value, or wealth.

Nudge: To gently and indirectly suggest alternatives that modify our attention and focus on a better choice without using penalties or coercion.

Offensive: Type of financial strategy that uses your strengths, assertiveness, and proactivity to increase your net financial position.

Opportunity cost: The same money spent for one purpose could have been used for something else with different benefits.

Ostrich effect: Being able to see what is in front of you while ignoring what would otherwise be an obviously negative or poor choice or circumstance.

Overcoming objections: A tactic used by salespeople to negate or discount your doubts to a purchase by appealing to your emotions.

Overconfidence bias: A behavioral trap where you are excessively confident, so much so that you make riskier or unwise choices.

Outcome: The result of a choice.

Outcome bias: When we evaluate if our decision was satisfactory based only on the outcome or result rather than assessing it based on what we knew at the time the choice was made.

Patterns: Consistent paths and become engrained in the way we unconsciously or subconsciously just do certain things.

Portfolio: An assortment of stocks, mutual funds, or other investment that helps to improve diversification.

Positivity effect: A behavioral bias in which we tend to favor and recall positive responses more readily than negative ones.

Power of attorney (POA): A legal document that assigns somebody else to have authority over making specific kinds of decisions when you become unable to perform certain duties

Present bias: A situation in which we more heavily weight those alternatives with a smaller benefit or payout "today" rather than a potentially bigger benefit in the future.

Principal: Initial money invested into an asset.

Procrastination bias: The tendency to avoid or put off activities which are unpleasant.

Prospect theory: A concept in behavioral economics in which decisions are not always optimal and are directly related to how the choice is framed for the decision-maker.

Psychology: The mental functions performed by the mind and brain.

Qualified plan: An employer-sponsored retirement plan that meets Internal Revenue Service criteria to receive special tax treatment, allowing tax deferrals of retirement contributions.

Quest: A journey or mission towards a (financial) destination that is difficult to find. The search for something meaningful.

Rational: Utilizing reason by understanding a problem, analyzing alternatives, and seeking out the best solution. Contemplation and consideration of alternatives and consequences.

Rational choice: Attempt to understand a problem and find an optimal solution. Logical, sensible, well-though out.

Reactive: Impulsive. Quick judgmental responses rather than through contemplation.

Reasoning: Contemplation and consideration of alternatives and consequences.

Recall bias: Our inability to remember accurately and completely what we did in the past.

Risk: Potential for loss. Uncertainty. Chance that something bad or negative will happen.

Risk aversion: The preference for certainty over any uncertainty, which causes us to alter behaviors because of perceptions.

Risk-free rates: The (low) rate of return you might expect on something with absolutely no risk. Generally, treasury bonds or US-backed securities.

Robo-investor: Use of technology that uses your preferences to determine optimal investment allocations and recommendations.

Roth IRA: A specific form of individual retirement account that uses after-tax investments and typically grows tax-free. Must meet specific Internal Revenue Service guidelines.

Scarcity: A money mindset characterized by lack of resources. Opposite of abundance.

Scenario planning: Involves making assumptions and estimates of potential future states at different points in the future to help prepare a contingency plan if the event comes true.

Self-serving bias: When we take credit for good choices but blame others for the poor ones.

Sequencing: The properly ordered financial moves necessary to achieve wealth.

Simulation model: Mathematical technique used on a computer that can predict performance given certain assumptions.

Speculation: Suggests that while we hope or expect an incremental return in the future, it is not a given, since there is risk involved.

Status quo bias: Becoming comfortable with how things exist today and not willing to make changes.

Stochastic: Choice in which uncertainty makes the outcome less predictable.

Stock: An ownership position (through shares) in a company.

Stereotype: A thought or idea about something (or someone) without actually knowing.

Substitution: A strategy for replacing one more positive habit for a negative financial habit.

Sunk cost: An expense that has already incurred and cannot be reversed.

Tax-deferred: The postponement of taxes incurred, including income and capital gains, until a later point in time. Typically refers to retirement planning in which qualified plans allow for tax deferral.

Time dependency: Separating the current moment from the best solution.

Trust: An arrangement in which you authorize somebody to hold and distribute assets to the beneficiaries you choose upon your death.

Umbrella insurance: Coverage for excess claims for property damage, personal liability, or lawsuits.

Uncertainty: Lack of something being known and familiar due, making choices less clear. Risk of loss.

Unconscious: When we make decisions automatically using autonomic processes within the nervous system. Autopilot.

Utility: Benefits derived from decisions.

Variability: Potential for change. Lack of stability or consistency.

Visioning: A process of imagination or goal setting.

Volatility: Unpredictable change. See variability.

Vulnerable: Exposed and open to receiving feedback and assistance.

Wealth: The abundance of financial resources. Financial health. Associated with an opportunistic, abundant, confident money mindset.

Wealth management: An active, mindful process of growing, preserving, and controlling our financial resources over the long term through mindful and consistent financial decisions.

Why: A purpose that is compelling and aspirational.

Will: Legal document that provides instructions on who and how to distribute certain assets

Appendix B: Useful Links and Resources

Sites to search for best interest rates (for homes and bank accounts)

- Bankrate — bankrate.com
- Money — money.com/best-savings-accounts
- High-yield savings — money.usnews.com/banking/high-yield-savings-accounts

Practical Government Sites

- Consumer finance — consumerfinance.gov/consumer-tools/retirement
- Medicare (annual enrollment) — medicare.gov
- Social Security (retirement) — ssa.gov

Credit Bureaus

- Annualcreditreport.com — A free service for all three credit bureaus, once per year
- Equifax.com
- Experian.com
- Transunion.com

Investment Research and Stock News

- Bloomberg — bloomberg.com
- CNBC — cnbc.com
- Fool — fool.com

■ FINRA	finra.org/investors
■ Forbes	forbes.com
■ Investopedia	investopedia.com
■ Investor's Business Daily	investors.com
■ Kiplinger Magazine	kiplinger.com
■ MarketWatch	marketwatch.com
■ Morningstar	morningstar.com
■ Wall Street Journal	wsj.com
■ Yahoo	finance.yahoo.com

Useful Financial Calculators

■ Future values with compound interest
  - investor.gov/financial-tools-calculators/calculators/compound-interest-calculator
■ Debt repayment calculator
  - https://www.creditkarma.com/calculators/debtrepayment
■ Retirement Calculator
  - https://investor.vanguard.com/calculator-tools/retirement-income-calculator
■ Mortgage Loan Amortization Calculators
  - mortgagecalculator.org

Major Investment Institutions

■ Betterment	betterment.com
■ Charles Schwab	schwab.com
■ e-Trade	us.etrade.com
■ Fidelity Investments	fidelity.com
■ Merrill Lynch	ml.com
■ TD Ameritrade	tdameritrade.com
■ T Rowe Price	troweprice.com
■ Vanguard Investments	vanguard.com

Financial Tools for Parents of Young Children

■ Gohenry	gohenry.com
■ Greenlightcard	greenlightcard.com
■ Stash	stash.com

Sites to Help you Find a Financial Advisor

- SEC/FINRA   brokercheck.finra.org
- America College of Financial Services
  - youradvisorguide.com/find-a-professional
- CFP Board of Standards   letsmakeaplan.org

Interesting Financial and Mindfulness Podcasts

- Brendon Bouchard (habits) podcast
  - brendon.com/podcast
- Changeability podcast   brilliantlivinghq.com/
                                        changeability-podcast-2
- Dave Ramsey podcast   ramseysolutions.com
- Hidden Brain podcast   hiddenbrain.org
- Jill Schlesinger podcast   jillonmoney.com
- Money Guy podcast   moneyguy.com
- Planet Money podcast   npr.org/sections/money
- Smart Money   nerdwallet.com/blog/podcast
- Success Magazine   success.com/podcasts
- Your Money's Worth   kiplinger.com/podcast

Specialized Investment Apps

- Acorns: Save and Invest   acorns.com
- Betterment   betterment.com
- Robinhood   robinhood.com
- SoFI   sofi.com
- Stash   stash.com
- Webull   webull.com

Financial Tracking Tools and Apps

- Chime
- Goodbudget
- Mint
- Personal Capital
- Simplifi by Quicken
- EveryDollar (Ramsey Solutions)

References

[1] Zakrzewski, A., Carrubba, J., Frankle, D., Hardie, A., Kahlich, M., Kessler, D., Mende, M., Tang, T. and Xavier, A. (2021). *Global Wealth: The Future of Wealth Management—A CEO Agenda*, 20th Edition. Boston Consulting Group: Boston, MA.

[2] Kohler, T. A. (2021). *Ten Thousand Years of Inequality: The Archaeology of Wealth Differences*. University of Arizona Press: Tucson, AZ.

[3] Smith, A. (1776). *An Inquiry into the Nature and Causes of the Wealth of Nations*. University of Chicago Press: Chicago, IL.

[4] IMDb.com (2021). Wall Street, Movie Details. Available at www.imdb.com.

[5] Wolff, E. N. and Gittleman, M. (2011). Inheritances and the Distribution of Wealth. Bureau of Labor Statistics Working Paper #445. January 2011. U.S. Department of Labor.

[6] Yahoo Finance (2020). Lottery Winners Who Lost Everything. *Yahoo Finance*. Available at www.yahoo.com/now/23-lottery-winners-lost-millions-193539538.html. Accessed on September 2, 2021.

[7] Housel, M. (2020). *Psychology of Money: Timeless Lessons on Wealth, Greed, and Happiness*. Harriman House: Petersfield.

[8] Hogan, C. (2019). *Everyday Millionaires*. Ramsey Press: Nashville, TN.

[9] CBS News (2019). Nearly One-Quarter of Americans Say They'll Never Retire, According to New Poll. July 8, 2019. Available at https://www.cbsnews.com/news/nearly-one-quarter-of-americans-say-theyll-never-retire-according-to-new-poll/. Accessed on September 1, 2021.

[10] Fox, M. (2019). 99% of Americans Don't Use a Financial Advisor—Here's Why. *CNBC*. November 11, 2019. Available at https://www.cnbc.com/2019/11/11/99percent-of-americans-dont-use-a-financial-advisor-heres-why.html.

[11] Levine, D. M., Linder, J. A. and Landon, B. E. (2020). Characteristics of Americans with Primary Care and Changes Over Time, 2002–2015. *JAMA Intern Med*, 180(3), 463–466.

[12] TransAmerica Center for Retirement (2020). Available at https://money.com/social-security-running-out-millennials.

[13] White, A. (2020). CNBC. Alaskans Carry the Highest Credit Card Balance—Here's the Average Credit Card Balance in Every State. December 1, 2020. Available at https://www.cnbc.com/select/average-credit-card-balance-by-state/.

[14] US Department of Education (2021). Federal Student Loan Portfolio. Available at https://studentaid.gov/data-center/student/portfolio. Accessed on April 27, 2021.

[15] Huddleston, C. (2019). Survey: 69% of Americans Have Less Than $1,000 in Savings. Available at https://www.gobankingrates.com/saving-money/savings-advice/americans-have-less-than-1000-in-savings/.

[16] Kirkham, E. (2016). 1 in 3 Americans Has Saved $0 for Retirement. March 14, 2016. Available at https://money.com/retirement-savings-survey/.

[17] Picketty, T. (2020). *Capital and Ideology*. Belknap Press/Harvard University Press: Cambridge, MA.

[18] Howe, N. (2018). The Graying of Wealth. *Forbes*. March 16, 2018. Available at https://www.forbes.com/sites/neilhowe/2018/03/16/the-graying-of-wealth/?sh=3036d55b302d.

[19] Brown, D. A. (2021). *The Whiteness of Wealth: How the Tax System Impoverishes Black Americans—and How We Can Fix It*. Crown Publishers: New York.

[20] Boenigk, S. and Mayr, M. L. (2016). The Happiness of Giving: Evidence from the German Socioeconomic Panel That Happier People Are More Generous. *J. Happiness Stud*, 17(5), 1825–1846.

[21] Brooks, A. C. (2007). Does Giving Make Us Prosperous? *J Econ Finan*, 31, 403–411.

[22] Leimberg, S., Jackson, M. and Satinsky, M. (2019). *The Tools & Techniques of Financial Planning*, 13th Edition. The National Underwriter Company, Kentucky.

[23] Eagleman, D. (2020). *Livewired: The Inside Story of the Ever-Changing Brain*. Vintage Books/Knopf Doubleday Publishing: New York, NY.

[24] Vokytek, B. (2013). Are There Really as Many Neurons in the Human Brain as Stars in the Milky Way? *Nature*, May 30, 2013. Available at https://www.nature.com/scitable/blog/brain-metrics/are_there_really_as_many/.

[25] Churchland, P. S. and Sejnowski, T. J. (1999). *The Computational Brain*. MIT Press: Cambridge, MA.

[26] Kahneman, D. (2011). *"Chapter 35. Two Selves." Thinking, Fast and Slow*. Farrar, Straus & Giroux: New York.

[27] Simon, H. (1957). A Behavioral Model of Rational Choice,". In *Models of Man, Social and Rational: Mathematical Essays on Rational Human Behavior in a Social Setting*. Wiley: New York.

[28] Likierman, A. (2020). The Elements of Good Judgment. *Harvard Business Review*. Available at https://hbr.org/2020/01/the-elements-of-good-judgment.

[29] Frydman, C. and Camerer, C. F. (2016). The Psychology and Neuroscience of Financial Decision-making. *Trends in Cognitive Sciences*, 20(9), 661–675.

[30] Tversky, A. and Kahneman, D. (1974). Judgment under Uncertainty: Heuristics and Biases. *Science*, 185(4157) (September 27), 1124–1131.

[31] Kahneman, D. and Tversky, A. (1979). Prospect Theory: An Analysis of Decision under Risk. *Econometrica*, 47(2), 263–291. doi:10.2307/1914185.

[32] Kahneman, D. (2011). *Thinking, Fast and Slow*. Penguin Publishers: New York, NY.

[33] Simon, H. (1955). A Behavioral Model of Rational Choice. *Quarterly Journal of Economics*, 69(1), 99–118.

[34] Honda, K. (2019). *Happy Money: The Japanese Art of Making Peace with Your Money.* Gallery Books: New York, NY.

[35] Langabeer, J. and DelliFraine, J. (2011). Does CEO Optimism Affect Strategic Process? *Management Research Review*, 34(8), 857–868.

[36] Thaler, R. and Sunstein, C. (2021). *Nudge: The Final Edition.* Penguin Books: New York, NY.

[37] Barnett Lisa, F. (2018). *How Emotions Are Made: The Secret Life of the Brain.* Houghton Mifflin Harcourt Publishing: Boston.

[38] De Couck, M., Caers, R., Musch, L., Fliegauf, J., Giangreco, A. and Gidron, Y. (2019). How Breathing Can Help You Make Better Decisions: Two Studies on the Effects of Breathing Patterns on Heart Rate Variability and Decision-Making in Business Cases. *Int J Psychophysiol*, 139 (May), 1–9.

[39] Markovitz, H. (1952). Portfolio Selection." *The Journal of Finance*, 7(1) (March), 77–91.

[40] Miller, M. H. and Modigliani, F. (1958). The Cost of Capital, Corporate Finance and the Theory of Investment,". *The American Economic Review*, XLVIII (June 3), 261–297.

[41] Stanley, T. J. and Danko, W. D. (2010). *The Millionaire Next Door: The Surprising Secrets of America's Wealthy.* Taylor Trade Publishing: Lanham, MD.

[42] Ricciardi, V. (2008). *The Psychology of Risk: The Behavioral Finance Perspective. Handbook of Finance: Volume 2, Investment Management and Financial Management*, F. J. Fabozzi (ed.). John Wiley & Sons: Hoboken, NJ, pp. 85–111.

[43] Pratt, J. (1964). Risk Aversion in the Small and in the Large. *Econometrica*, 32(1/2), 122–136. doi:10.2307/1913738.

[44] Martin, E. CNBC (2019). The Government Shutdown Spotlights a Bigger Issue: 78% of US Workers Live Paycheck to Paycheck. Available at https://www.cnbc.com/2019/01/09/shutdown-highlights-that-4-in-5-us-workers-live-paycheck-to-paycheck.html.

[45] Definition of Commitment (2021). Merriam Webster Dictionary. Available at https://www.merriam-webster.com/dictionary/commitment. Accessed on September 2, 2021.

[46] Huston, S. J. (2010). Measuring Financial Literacy. *Journal of Consumer Sciences*, 44(2), 296–315.

[47] Jappelli, T. and Padulo, M. (2013). Investment in Financial Literacy and Saving Decisions. *Journal of Banking and Finance*, 37(8), 2779–2792.

[48] Behrman, J. R., Mitchell, O. S., Soo, C. K. and Bravo, D. (2012). How Financial Literacy Affects Household Wealth Accumulation. *American Economic Review*, 102(3), 300–304.

[49] Madrian, B. and Shea, D. (2001). The Power of Suggestion: Inertia in 401(k) Participation and Savings Behavior. *Quarterly Journal of Economics*, 116, 1149–1187.

[50] Definition of Mindful (2021). Cambridge Dictionary. Available at https://dictionary.cambridge.org/us/dictionary/english/mindful. Accessed on September 9, 2021.

[51] Brown, B. (2015). *Daring Greatly: How the Courage to Be Vulnerable Transforms the Way We Live, Love, Parent, and Lead.* Avery-Penguin Books: New York, NY.

[52] Definition of Consciousness (2021). Cambridge English Dictionary. Available at dictionary.cambridge.org.

[53] Kabat-Zinn, J. (2005). *Wherever You Go, There You Are: Mindfulness Meditation in Everyday Life*. Hachette Books: Paris.

[54] Tversky, A. and Kahneman, D. (1973). Availability: A Heuristic for Judging Frequency and Probability." *Cognitive Psychology*, 5(2) (September), 207–232.

[55] Marketwatch.com (2021). The 25 Largest Mutual Funds. Available at https://www.marketwatch.com/tools/mutual-fund/top25largest. Accessed on September 17, 2021.

[56] Bem, D. J. (1972). Self-perception Theory. *Advances in Experimental Social Psychology*, 6, 1–62.

[57] Clear, J. (2018). *Atomic Habits. An Easy & Proven Way to Build Good Habits & Break Bad Ones*. Avery-Penguin Books: New York, NY.

[58] Rubin, G. (2017). *The Four Tendencies: The Indispensable Personality Profiles That Reveal How to Make Your Life Better (and Other People's Lives Better, Too)*. Harmony Books, Crown Publishing Group: Danvers, MA.

[59] Certified Financial Planner Board of Standards, Inc (2021). Definition of Financial Planning. Available at cfp.net. Accessed on May 19, 2021.

[60] Dickler, J. (2019). 75 75 Percent of Americans Are Winging it When it Comes to Their Financial Future. Available at https://www.cnbc.com/2019/04/01/when-it-comes-to-their-financial-future-most-americans-are-winging-it.html. Accessed on September 15, 2021.

[61] Fazzi, R. (2021). Nearly Half of U.S. Adults See Advisors as Too Expensive, Magnify Money Says. *Financial Advisor Magazine*, May 12, 2021.

[62] Sinek, S., Mead, D. and Shledtzky, S. (2017). *Find Your Why: A Practical Guide for Discovering Purpose for You and Your Team*. Penguin Publishing: London.

[63] Shalley, C. E., Oldham, G. R. and Porac, J. F. (1987). Effects of Goal Difficulty, Goal-Setting Method, and Expected External Evaluation on Intrinsic Motivation. *Academy of Management Journal*, 30, 553–563.

[64] Wallace, S. G. and Etkin, J. (2018). How Goal Specificity Shapes Motivation: A Reference Points Perspective. *Journal of Consumer Research*, 44(5), 1033–1051.

[65] Internal Revenue Service (2021). Traditional and Roth IRAs. Available at https://www.irs.gov/retirement-plans/traditional-and-roth-iras. Accessed on September 15, 2021.

[66] Charles Schwab (2021). Survey of Modern Wealth. Available at www.aboutschwab.com/modern-wealth-survey-2021.

[67] Ebehardt, W., Bruine de Bruin, W. and Strough, J. (2018). Age Differences in Financial Decision-making. *Behavioral Decision-Making*, 32(1), 79–93.

[68] Gamble, K. J., Boyle, P. A., Yu, L. and Bennett, D. A. (2015). Aging and Financial Decision-making. *Management Science*, 61(11), 2603–2261.

[69] Agarwal, S., Driscoll, J. C., Gabaix, X. and Laibson, D. I. (2009). The Age of Reason: Financial Decisions Over the Life-Cycle with Implications for Regulation. *Brookings Papers on Economic Activity*, 40, 51–117.

[70] Smith, R. (2019). Baby Boomers' Biggest Financial Risk: Cognitive Decline. *Wall Street Journal*, June 6, 2019. Available at https://www.wsj.com/articles/baby-boomers-biggest-financial-risk-cognitive-decline-11622942343?mod=hp_jr_pos1.

[71] Stein Gertrude (1937). Everybody's Autobiography. *Random House Publishing.* page 289.

[72] Lovalio, D. and Sibony, O. (201). McKinsey Quarterly. *The Case for Behavioral Strategy*, March 1, 2010.

[73] Benscheidt, K. and Carpenter, J. (2020). Advanced Counter-Biasing. *Journal of Economic Behavior & Organization*, 177, 1–18.

[74] Sellier, A.-L., Scopelliti, I. and Morewedge, C. K. (2019). Debiasing Training Improves Decision-making in the Field. *Psychological Science*, August 7, 2019. Available at https://www.psychologicalscience.org/news/minds-business/debiasing-your-decisions.html.

[75] Hirshleifer, D., Levi, Y., Lourie, B. and Teoh, S. W. (2019). Decision Fatigue and Heuristic Analyst Forecasts. *Journal of Financial Economics*, 133(1), 83–98.

[76] Taibbi, R. (2019). Do You Have Analysis Paralysis? *Psychology Today*. Available at https://www.psychologytoday.com/us/blog/fixing-families/201904/do-you-have-analysis-paralysis. Accessed on September 14, 2021.

[77] Ferrari, J., Johnson, J. and McCown, W. (1995). *Procrastination and Task Avoidance Theory, Research, and Treatment. Springer Series in Social Clinical Psychology.* Springer Science: New York.

[78] Ariely, D. (2017). *Dollars and Sense: How We Misthink Money and How to Spend Smarter.* Harper Publishing: New York.

[79] Banker, S., Dunfield, D., Huang, A., et al. (2021). Neural Mechanisms of Credit Card Spending. *Sci Rep*, 11, 4070.

Index

Note: Page numbers in **bold** indicate definition of the term on the corresponding glossary page.